GLADIATOR

ROME'S BLOODY SPECTACLE

OSPREY
PUBLISHING

GLADIATOR

ROME'S BLOODY SPECTACLE

KONSTANTIN NOSSOV

First published in Great Britain in 2009 by Osprey Publishing,
Midland House, West Way, Botley, Oxford OX2 0PH, United Kingdom.
443 Park Avenue South, New York, NY 10016, USA.

Email: info@ospreypublishing.com

Previously published as *Gladiators: History, Types, Armament, Organisation of Spectacles* (St Petersburg,
"Atlant", 2005, in Russian.)
© 2009 Osprey Publishing Ltd
Text © 2009 Konstantin Nossov

A CIP catalogue record for this book is available from the British Library

ISBN: 978 1 84603 472 5

Konstantin Nossov has asserted his right under the Copyright, Designs and Patents Act, 1988,
to be identified as the author of this book.

With illustrations by Vladimir Golubev.

Page layout by Myriam Bell Design, France
Index by Fineline Editorial Services
Typeset in Centaur MT
Originated by PPS Grasmere, Leeds, UK
Printed in China through Worldprint

09 10 11 12 13   10 9 8 7 6 5 4 3 2 1

Front cover: istockphoto.com, artist Vladamir Golubev

For a catalogue of all books published by Osprey please contact:

NORTH AMERICA
Osprey Direct, c/o Random House Distribution Center
400 Hahn Road, Westminster, MD 21157, USA
E-mail: uscustomerservice@ospreypublishing.com

ALL OTHER REGIONS
Osprey Direct, The Book Service Ltd., Distribution Centre, Colchester Road, Frating Green,
Colchester, Essex, CO7 7DW
E-mail: customerservice@ospreypublishing.com

Osprey Publishing is supporting the Woodland Trust, the UK's leading woodland
conservation charity, by funding the dedication of trees.

www.ospreypublishing.com

CONTENTS

PREFACE

The Russian version of this book came out in 2005. Since that time, various new historical works on the gladiators have been published, and this English edition has subsequently taken in the latest research. Moreover, I have given further serious consideration to the observations and advice of my gladiatorially focused colleagues. I should particularly like to single out I. V. Akilov. From his profound knowledge of the subject, he has suggested several promising fresh ideas, which are also reflected in this book.

I would like to take the opportunity to note the outstanding role played by the prominent German scholar Marcus Junkelmann in this field of study. He was the first to develop a harmonious classification system for the types of gladiators and their weapons, reconstructing many of the latter and throwing new light upon some old issues.

In the translation of the book into English, I have tried to use quotations from sources published in English-language editions. Unfortunately, not all sources are available in such translations. Therefore, I have sometimes given my own translations, sticking as far as possible to the language of the original. The same situation is reflected in the bibliography, where I did my best to list the English editions of primary sources; Russian and Latin editions will be found alongside each other, however. In the bibliography I sometimes cite two different editions for the same source, where the translations differ considerably but where I have made use of both versions.

To my great regret, not all first editions of contemporary foreign authors are available, even in the best Russian libraries. In these cases, I was obliged to refer to later editions, with their imprints noted in the bibliography. Furthermore, some of the works have been translated into Russian and I have not been able to find editions in the original language. Still, I have decided to retain references to these books, as I think it is better to have at least any reference than none at all.

Finally, I would like to express my sincere gratitude to Dr Michael Gorelik for his useful remarks and advice, as well as for some of the materials he kindly put at my disposal. I also thank my wife, Natalia Zaroshchinskaya, for her invaluable assistance in preparing the materials.

Konstantin Nossov
September 2008

INTRODUCTION

Gladiators were famously popular in ancient Rome for seven centuries, from the 3rd century BC to the 4th century AD. They were hugely celebrated – commemorated in reliefs and numerous mosaics; reproduced in statuettes and on everyday objects; immortalized by fans who scrawled the names of favourite gladiators on the walls of buildings. Roman citizens testified to dreams of gladiators and gladiatorial combat, and there were books dedicated to interpreting such dreams.

After these eight glorious centuries, the gladiators faded into oblivion. From the 5th through to the mid-18th century, curiosity about the gladiators disappeared and probably very few people in the wider world knew anything about them. Yet in 1766 a new wave of interest in the their lives and actions arose when some gladiatorial weapons were found in Pompeii. Since that time the subject has never lost its appeal to historians and the public at large. The 19th century saw artworks and novels dedicated to gladiatorial themes, and the 20th century made them the central heroes of Hollywood movies.

We start our analysis with a basic question – what are gladiatorial games? Furthermore, in what way do they differ from, say, medieval tournaments, judicial duels, or simple armed clashes? How are we to interpret the gladiator phenomenon? The answers to these questions offer a starting point in our search for the origins of gladiatorial games and their subsequent spread.

At the outset, we need to clarify terminology. In ancient Rome, games accompanied by gladiatorial fighting were called *munus* (pl. *munera*), although today 'gladiatorial games' (the second word is often replaced by 'contest' or 'combat') is used as a blanket description, so the terms will be synonymous from here on. Gladiatorial combat (*munus*) can be defined in the following way: a fight between equally matched armed men before the eyes of spectators, in which the killing of the opponent was generally (although not always) the objective. The participants in such fights were called gladiators.

The difference between this combat and that of medieval tournaments is obvious – the death of an opponent was not the goal of the latter. Combatants at the tournament could leave the tiltyard at will, which gladiators could not do. As to duels (formalized combat between two individuals), they were not mass spectacles, but were fought by two men to settle a personal quarrel. Both tournaments and duels followed a code of honour, written or unwritten, which prohibited the killing of a wounded opponent – such was considered a despicable act. Gladiatorial fighting, by contrast, envisaged death as an outcome from the beginning, with the survival or demise of the defeated warrior depending wholly on the public's decision. There were also important social differences between gladiators and the later fighters. Only the elite, the higher nobility, enjoyed the privilege of taking part in tournaments and only noblemen could fight a duel (at least, using a 'noble' weapon, not just fists or sticks). As for gladiators, they were slaves or criminals or prisoners of war; citizens who became gladiators of their own free will were deprived of all their rights and despised by their fellow countrymen.

Closest to gladiatorial combat was the judicial duel (also known as 'trial by combat'), seen in Europe from around the 9th to the 16th century, in which two parties in legal dispute fought in single combat. The defeated was to plead guilty or die, while the winner of the fight was legally vindicated and declared innocent. A judicial duel was fought with real weapons, as a rule, and in the presence of spectators. So the three basic rules of gladiatorial contest – the use of real weapons, the presence of the public and a frequently fatal outcome – were often observed at judicial duels, too. The difference, however, is that the duels were not arranged as public enjoyment, but as an act of legal procedure dedicated to God, and it was not the public but the victor who decided whether the defeated should live or die.

In other societies, gladiatorial-style combat was a way of making human sacrifices. Such was seen among the Aztec civilization – a prisoner was given a blunt weapon to fight against four opponents armed with sharp weapons of war.[1] In contrast with gladiatorial games, however, here the combatants were decidedly and deliberately unequal, so the outcome of the combat was pre-determined. It was essentially nothing but an execution.

The Roman gladiatorial games comprised both single combat and team fighting. Somewhat at a tangent, Roman games also included beast hunts and mock naval battles, which were called *venatio* and *naumachia* respectively. Like the execution of unarmed criminals in the arena, *venatio* and *naumachia* do not strictly fall under the definition of gladiatorial games, although they often accompanied the latter. Therefore *munus*, *venatio* and *naumachia* are all examined in the book. The execution of prisoners is only touched in passing, as a part of spectacle. Chariot races, boxing matches, athletic competitions and other performances frequently given in Rome deserve to be examined separately and are not considered here.

CHAPTER I

THE HISTORY OF ROMAN SPECTACLES

GLADIATORIAL GAMES

Gladiatorial games, like many other Roman customs, were long considered to have come from the Etruscans.[2] Yet not one surviving Etruscan artefact offers direct evidence of gladiatorial contests in Etruria. Mural paintings in the tombs of Etruscan nobility represent various sport activities, such as chariot races and athletic contests, for instance, but there are no gladiatorial combats among them. The famous drawing in the Augures' Tomb in the city of Tarquinia shows a hooded man armed with a stick defending himself against a dog, which has been set on him by a man whose face is covered with a mask. It is, however, a beast attacking a man, not two men fighting in the arena, so it cannot be considered as gladiatorial fighting.

A revolution in understanding gladiatorial origins came with the recent discovery of frescos in Campania, southern Italy. Most of the frescos were found at Paestum, to the south-east of Naples. They date from 370–340 BC and depict various scenes of funeral games: chariot races, boxing matches and — what is most important for us — single combat between two fighters armed with spears, both holding shields and wearing helmets. Sometimes guards can be seen behind the fighting men, which suggests that it was a forced combat. The fighters often have bleeding wounds and one of the frescos seems to depict the killing of an opponent.[3] Here we find direct parallels with the Roman *munera*. Unfortunately we know nothing of the combatants — were they prisoners of war or criminals, had they been specially trained for combat or just chosen at the last moment?

Above and right: Two frescos representing *bustuarii* gladiators, from graves in Paestum, Campania. Both frescos date from the mid-4th century BC. (Museo Archeologico Nazionale, Paestum)

Further convincing evidence of the Campanian origin of the gladiatorial games is given by Livy. In 308 BC, in the course of the Second Samnite War (327–304 BC), the Romans won a decisive victory over the Samnites. They took a lot of armour as a trophy and used it to decorate their forum, while 'the Campanians, out of contempt and hatred towards the Samnites, made the gladiators who performed at their banquets wear it, and they then called them "Samnites"'.[4]

It would appear that gladiatorial combat was already well known in Campania by 308 BC. Some other facts seem to suggest a Campanian origin to the gladiatorial games: it was here that the first stone amphitheatres were built, and that the most famous gladiatorial schools were subsequently situated. The Romans, who had maintained close contacts with Capua (the centre of Campania), in turn could not have been unaware of the gladiators, although the Romans might have become acquainted with gladiatorial combat through the Etruscans, who in turn learned them from the Campanians.[5]

The first mention of a gladiatorial combat in Rome dates back to 264 BC, when two sons of the deceased D. Junius Brutus Pera brought out three pairs of gladiators at the funeral games to honour their father.[6] The custom of spilling human blood on the grave of a deceased relative was an ancient one, characteristic of most ancient Mediterranean cultures. Blood was believed to reconcile the dead with the living. Human sacrifices had been known in Rome before this date, but here was the first known occasion in the city where gladiatorial combat was staged at a funeral. Previously, in their hope to placate the deceased with human blood, the Romans sacrificed prisoners of war or unfortunate slaves; now they decided to add some pleasure to the process in the form of gladiatorial fighting.[7] The next reference to gladiatorial contests in Rome dates to 216 BC, when three sons of Markus Aemilius Lepidus arranged funeral games in honour of their father and brought out 22 pairs of gladiators onto the forum.[8] Although there is no evidence of gladiatorial combat taking place in Rome between these two dates, they undoubtedly did take place, at least at the funeral games in honour of distinguished Roman citizens.

Carthaginians are also known to have held gladiatorial games. At the very beginning of the Second Punic War (218–202 BC), Hannibal attempted to boost the morale of his army by having captured mountain people fight each other using Gallic weapons. The prize-winner was to receive his freedom, as well as armour and a horse. Every prisoner was eager to try his luck:

> When they began to fight such was the state of feeling not only amongst the men who had accepted this condition, but amongst the spectators generally, that the good fortune of those who died bravely was lauded quite as much as that of those who were victorious. After his men had been impressed by watching several pairs of combatants Hannibal dismissed them.[9]

More unusual gladiatorial combats were staged by the Roman commander and statesman Scipio, *c.* 206 BC, in New Carthage, Spain, in memory of his father and uncle:

> The gladiators on this occasion were not drawn from the class from which the trainers usually take them – slaves and men who sell their blood – but were all volunteers and gave their services gratuitously. Some had been sent by their chiefs to give an exhibition of the instinctive courage of their race, others professed their willingness to fight out of compliment to their general, others again were drawn by a spirit of rivalry to challenge one another to single combat. There were several who had outstanding quarrels with one another and who agreed to seize this opportunity of deciding them by the sword on the agreed condition that the vanquished was to be at the disposal of the victor. [10]

Even two noble cousins, Corbis and Orsua, came out into the arena to decide, with weapons, their argument about supremacy over the city of Ibes.

It is apparent that gladiatorial combat was already common by 206 BC, and not only slaves but free citizens took part. Over time, the numbers of fighters engaged in gladiatorial contests increased. In 183 BC, the funeral games in honour of Publius Licinius included 60 pairs of fighters,[11] while in 174 BC Titus Flamininus presented 74 gladiators at the death of his father.[12] The latter games, accompanied by feasting (plus the free distribution of meat) and plays, lasted four days, with three days allotted for gladiatorial combat.

Public games (*ludi*) were organized by state officials and included theatrical performances and chariot races, but originally did not include gladiatorial combat. As we have seen, gladiators mainly featured in funeral games in honour of powerful Romans. As a rule, a noble Roman would leave an instruction as to how his funeral should be organized. His will had the status of law for his heirs, who used the opportunity to demonstrate the wealth and power of their family. That is why gladiatorial fights acquired the name *munus*, from the Latin meaning 'obligation' or 'gift'. Gladiators fighting to commemorate the deceased were called *bustuarii* (from the Latin *bustum* – 'funeral fire'). They did not fight in front of the grave itself, but instead did so at funeral games specially arranged for the ninth day after the funeral, when the formal period of grief generally ended.[13]

On occasions, the deceased left a fairly extravagant will that placed his heirs in an awkward position. For instance, the will of one distinguished Roman stipulated that beautiful girls were to be combatants at his own funeral games, while another nobleman stated that the boys with whom he had a pederastic relationship should fight against each other. In the latter case, however, the public indignantly rejected the dead man's wish.[14]

During the 2nd century BC, gladiatorial combat spread all over Italy. From a religious rite they gradually transformed into a means of political influence over the people. The deceased sometimes had to wait rather a long time for their wills to be carried out, as the heir tried to time *munus* to coincide strategically with the next elections. Thus Julius Caesar, hoping for the position of edile, opened gladiatorial games in honour of his father 20 years after the latter's death.[15] State-financed gladiatorial combats were first conducted in 44 BC on the occasion of Caesar's death, not in 105 BC as was believed earlier.[16] (In 105 BC, the first fencing instructors from gladiatorial schools were recruited for training legionaries.) During the age of the Roman Empire, furthermore, *munera* would acquire a more secular character.

It was probably via Roman traditions that the custom of funerary gladiatorial combat was occasionally observed by other peoples. Gladiatorial fights were held in 139 BC at the funeral of Viriathus, leader of the rebellious anti-Roman Lusitani, a Celtic people that lived on the territory of modern Portugal.[17] Germans staged single-combat events with weapons, obviously resembling gladiatorial fights, in order to obtain favour from the gods: 'Another kind of divination, by which they explore the event of momentous wars, is to oblige a prisoner, taken by any means whatsoever from the nation with whom they are at variance, to fight with a picked man of their own, each with his own country's arms; and, according as the victory falls, they presage success to the one or to the other party.'[18]

Gladiatorial games were held by the Syrian king Antiochus IV Epiphanes (215–163 BC). He had long been kept a hostage in Rome, where he probably witnessed these spectacles. Back in Syria, in 175 BC, he seized the throne and began to put on gladiatorial contests based on the Roman model, at first inviting professional gladiators from Rome. At first, the public, unaccustomed to such sights, was horrified, but 'by frequently giving these exhibitions, in which the gladiators sometimes only wounded one another, and at other times fought to the death, he familiarised the eyes of his people to them and they learnt to enjoy them. In this way he created amongst most of the younger men a passion for arms.'[19]

If politicians entertained the common people with splendid *munera* in an attempt to attract support for a forthcoming election, the people returned the debt in kind.

Early in the 1st century AD, the inhabitants of Pollentia (Pollenza) in Liguria prevented a procession carrying the remains of a senior centurion from leaving the town square until they had forced the heirs to pay a large sum of money for gladiatorial games.[20] Two cohorts hurriedly moved to Pollentia to punish the citizens, but the fact remains that gladiatorial games had already become the cultural flesh and blood of the Roman people, who now believed in their right to demand them.

In 73 BC there occurred an event that threw Roman society into horror. Some 70 gladiators led by the infamous Spartacus killed their guards and ran away from Lentulus Batiatus' gladiatorial school in Capua. At first the Roman authorities attached no great importance to the breakout. However, as numerous slaves joined the escaped gladiators the fugitive band grew to several thousand men strong and began to win one victory after another over the Roman legions. The detachments that separated from Spartacus' army were less lucky, though; they were all quickly destroyed by Roman troops. That was how Crixus, Spartacus' comrade-in-arms in the gladiator school and a commander in the slave army, was killed. Spartacus provided a funeral in true Roman style — 300 imprisoned Roman legionaries fought as gladiators at the games held in Crixus' honour. At first, the slave army moved to Gallia, intending to leave Italy and return home, but then they changed direction for no obvious reason and turned south. The news of the slave army heading for Rome plunged the city's inhabitants into panic. Spartacus, however, ignored the Eternal City and crossed Italy from north to south (from Gallia Cisalpina to Bruttium). Only in 71 BC did Marcus Crassus lead the Roman army to a decisive victory in this Third Servile War or 'Gladiator War'.[21] Although this gladiatorial insurrection was not the only one in the Roman history, it was unique in terms of its grand scale. At last the Romans realized how dangerous slaves led by a handful of gladiators could be.

The number of gladiatorial fighters sent into the arena increased dramatically in the 1st century BC. *Munus* occasionally lasted many days or even months, with hundreds or thousands of participants. In 65 BC, Julius Caesar brought out 320 pairs of fighters,[22] probably from his own school in Capua, where 5,000 gladiators underwent concurrent training. He was also the first to give games in the honour of his daughter (previously funerary combats were only given in honour of a father), at which, side by side with professional gladiators, Furius Leptinus of a praetorian family (a praetor was an important Roman magistrate) and Quintus Calpenus, an ex-senator and a pleader of causes, fought to the death.[23] Moreover, at the festivities on the occasion of his triumph in the civil war in 46 BC, Julius Caesar staged a battle between two detachments, each consisting of 500 infantrymen, 20 war elephants and 30 cavalry. The battle took place in a circus, where two camps were built. The goals were even removed for lack of space.[24] (The circus was a structure designed primarily for chariot races, although other competitions were also held there. Two goals — *meta prima* and *meta secunda* — were put at the ends of the ground and the racing chariots had to pass around these goals.)

The Imperial period is rightly considered to be the golden age of gladiatorial games. Emperor Augustus (r. 27 BC–AD 14) had the greatest impact on the reorganization of gladiatorial games. He strictly regulated the types of gladiators and their weapons, introduced fighting rules and even allocated different standards of seating for the representatives of different social classes. His rule was commemorated by a great number of gladiatorial contests, *venatio* and a grandiose *naumachia*: 'In the number, variety, and magnificence of his public spectacles, he surpassed all former example.'[25] Augustus himself testified:

> Three times I gave shows of gladiators under my name and five times under the name of my sons and grandsons; in these shows about 10,000 men fought. Twice I furnished under my name spectacles of athletes gathered from everywhere, and three times under my grandson's name. I celebrated games under my name four times, and furthermore in the place of other magistrates twenty-three times... Twenty-six times, under my name or that of my sons and grandsons, I gave the people hunts of African beasts in the circus, in the open, or in the amphitheatre; in them about 3,500 beasts were killed.[26]

All in all, Emperor Augustus recruited 10,000 participants at eight great gladiatorial games, with more than 1,000 gladiators featured in each *munus*. Such grandiose *munera* were uncommon even in the city of Rome, to say nothing of smaller Italian cities or provinces, where just 20–50 pairs of gladiators typically engaged in a *munus*, with an average of 12–13 pairs a day appearing in the arena.

Augustus' successor Tiberius (r. AD 14–37) disliked gladiatorial games and rarely staged them.[27] When he did, however, the games were notable for their splendour, and even retired gladiators (*rudiarii*) were invited back into the arena to reap a reward of 100,000 sesterces.[28] Caligula (r. 37–41[29]) staged gladiatorial games either in Statilius Taurus' amphitheatre or in the Saepta civic building, both in Rome.[30] This bloodthirsty and cruel emperor turned the games into an outright slaughter, with innocent men from slaves to senators brought out onto the arena floor. One day he ordered Esius Proculus, the son of a centurion of the first rank, notable for his enormous height and handsome appearance, to be brought to the arena and fought him against two gladiators, one after another. He was victorious in both combats, but Caligula had him dragged in rags along the streets before he was butchered. Without even examining their supposed offences, Caligula also fed numerous prisoners to wild animals in the amphitheatre. The same lot befell a Roman of the equestrian class. Another wretch, the author of an controversial verse, was publicly burned to death in an amphitheatre. Should a member of the nobility criticize the games, he could find himself being sentenced to work in the mines or on the roads, or fed to beasts or cut in half with a saw.[31]

Claudius (r. 41–54) maintained a high frequency of gladiatorial games. They were celebrated modestly in a praetorian camp or pompously in the Saepta. He sometimes gave a show without preliminary advertisements – he called this *sportula*, of similar meaning to the French *hors d'oeuvre*, as the 'entertaining was unexpected and unprepared'. At the performances his manner was affable and simple: 'insomuch that he would hold out his left hand, and joined by the common people, count upon his fingers aloud the gold pieces presented to those who came off conquerors. He would earnestly invite the company to be merry; sometimes calling them his "masters", with a mixture of insipid, far-fetched jests.'[32] In time, however, Claudius manifested sadistic inclinations similar to Caligula's. He enjoyed looking into the faces of dying people so much that would order the final blow dealt even to gladiators who had simply fallen over, and especially to *retiarii* fighters (see below), who fought with their faces exposed. Moreover, like his predecessor he sent people to fight in the arena for the slimmest reasons or without any reason at all – for example, labourers could find themselves fighting to the death if construction did not meet expected standards.[33]

Celebrating the victory in Britain in 44, Claudius presented on the Field of Mars (Campus Martius) 'the assault and sacking of a town, and the surrender of the British kings, presiding in his general's cloak.'[34] Several more such team battles are known, including the one organized by Julius Caesar in 46 BC, mentioned above. In 7 BC, the Saepta witnessed another immense slaughter in honour of statesman and general Agrippa, who had died five years earlier. Smaller-scale battles were staged by Nero (r. 54–58) in 57 in the arena of an amphitheatre and by Domitian (r. 81–96) in a circus.[35] After he seized Jerusalem in 70, the future emperor Titus (r. 79–81) put on team combats between imprisoned Jews in honour of his brother's birthday.[36]

Professional gladiators did not fight in the large battles – the numerous performers in such events were criminals sentenced to death (*noxii*) or prisoners. Executions of criminals usually took place in the arena about noon or during a midday break. This is how Seneca described one such massacre:

By chance I attended a mid-day exhibition, expecting some fun, wit, and relaxation, – an exhibition at which men's eyes have respite from the slaughter of their fellow-men. But it was quite the reverse. The previous combats were the essence of compassion; but now all the trifling is put aside and it is pure murder. The men have no defensive armour. They are exposed to blows at all points, and no one ever strikes in vain. Many persons prefer this programme to the usual pairs and to the bouts 'by request'. Of course they do; there is no helmet or shield to deflect the weapon. What is the need of defensive armour, or of skill? All these mean delaying death. In the morning they throw men to the lions and the bears; at noon, they throw

Gladiatorial combats. In the top relief from left to right are two equites, a *myrmillo–hoplomachus* pair (two umpires can be seen behind them) and a *thraex–myrmillo* pair. The bottom relief (from left to right) shows *thraex–myrmillo, myrmillo–thraex, myrmillo–hoplomachus* and *thraex–myrmillo* pairs. 2nd quarter of the 1st century AD, featured on Lusius Storax's tombstone. (Museo Archeologico 'La Civitella', Chieti)

them to the spectators. The spectators demand that the slayer shall face the man who is to slay him in his turn; and they always reserve the latest conqueror for another butchering. The outcome of every fight is death, and the means are fire and sword. This sort of thing goes on while the arena is empty.[37]

In 69, Vitellius (r. September–December 69) hurried to celebrate his birthday 'by holding gladiatorial shows in every quarter of Rome on a scale of magnificence hitherto unknown'[38] – there were 265 quarters in Rome at that time. Vitellius was unable to neglect entertainment even at the height of a civil war, and he used his legions to build new amphitheatres for gladiatorial games.[39]

Emperor Titus celebrated the opening of the Colosseum in 80 with magnificent 100-day festivities lasting from June until September, and which included *munera*, *venatio* and *naumachia*. Unfortunately, nothing particular is known about the gladiatorial contests, as the contemporaries were more impressed by *venatio* and *naumachia* (see below).

According to Suetonius, Domitian (r. 81–96) 'frequently entertained the people with most magnificent and costly shows, not only in the amphitheatre, but also in the circus.'[40] In particular, Suetonius describes chariot races, gladiatorial combat, wild animal baiting and *naumachia*. Domitian enjoyed watching night-time beast chasing and gladiatorial fighting. Women were also participants in these events.[41] Combat between dwarves was also popular at this time. During quaestors' games (quaestors were officials with responsibilities for finances, amongst other affairs), Domitian 'always gave the people the liberty of demanding two pair of gladiators out of his own school, who appeared last of all, wearing court uniforms.'[42] Domitian was eventually assassinated, and ironically there were gladiators from his own school among the conspirators.[43]

In 107, Emperor Trajan (r. 98–117) delivered magnificent games on the occasion of a victory over the Dacians. He obviously wished to surpass Titus in terms of spectacle – during the 120-day games (Titus' games lasted 100 days), 10,000 gladiators were engaged in combat and 11,000 animals were killed.[44] Trajan staged three more gladiatorial games in the following five years: 350 men featured in the first, 'only' 202 in the second, and the third, lasting 117 days, delivered 4,941 pairs to fight in the arena.[45] In all, nearly 20,500 gladiators performed in the Roman arena between the years 107 and 113.

While Hadrian (r. 117–38) enjoyed gladiatorial games and beast baiting,[46] Marcus Aurelius (r. 161–80) disliked this entertainment. He attended such events reluctantly and even set a limit on the money spent on gladiatorial games.[47]

Moreover, he called gladiators to military service during times of war, causing discontent among the common people.[48] Unlike Marcus Aurelius, his co-ruler Lucius Verus (r. 161–69) adored watching gladiatorial fights, particularly during his feasts.[49] The same is true of Elagabalus (r. 218–22), famed in history for his extreme perversion: 'Before a banquet he would frequently watch gladiatorial fights and boxing matches, and he had a couch spread for himself in an upper gallery and during luncheon exhibited criminals in a wild-beast hunt.'[50] He apparently enjoyed this 'entertainment', at the same time as indulging his gluttony in the small, specially built amphitheatre of Castrense (see Chapter 5).

No emperor can compare with Commodus (r. 180–92) in his love of gladiatorial games. There is even a hypothesis that he was really the son of a gladiator, as his mother Faustina was not known for her loyalty to her husband Marcus Aurelius and obviously had a soft spot for gladiators.[51] Ruthless and bloodthirsty, Commodus delighted in killing both people and animals. He slaughtered thousands of animals in the arena as well as in his own house, and always did it himself. Gifted with impressive strength, Commodus practised killing different animals at one stroke and is even said to have been able to down an elephant with a spear strike.

Fighting with gladiators in the arena, Commodus gained about 1,100 victories, 365 of them when Marcus Aurelius was alive and 735 after his death. He enjoyed killing *retiarii* (a shieldless gladiator armed with a net, trident and dagger): playing the part of a *secutor* (the *retiarus'* opponent), he armed himself accordingly and only threw a small purple scrap of cloth on his shoulders as a distinguishing feature. He was very proud of his performances in the amphitheatre and demanded that official documents should always contain information about his participation. He was especially happy to be given the nickname 'Captain of the *Secutores*', which he was awarded 620 times. Furthermore, he was glad to be called by the name of a famous gladiator and not averse to having a drink with gladiators. There were no limits in his shamelessness – he appeared in women's dresses in the boxes of theatres and amphitheatres, and one day even came out into the arena completely naked, only a weapon in his hand.[52] He was so fond of gladiatorial games that at one point he even thought of taking up residence in a gladiators' barracks.[53] Despite his love of gladiatorial combat, Commodus was killed at home, not in the arena as shown in the well-known Hollywood blockbuster *Gladiator* (2000). He was strangled by an athlete who was his usual training partner.

The final stage of a combat supposedly between a *myrmillo* and a *thraex*. Relief from Ephesus, Asia Minor, 3rd century AD. (Antikensammlung, Staatliche Muzeen zu Berlin, SK 964. Author's collection)

As an edile (an office responsible for public buildings, festivals and public order), Gordian I (r. 238) paid for 12 games, one every month. On occasions he presented 500 pair of gladiators, and never less than 150.[54] When Maximus and Balbinus were appointed emperors in 238, and before the army was sent to war against Maximinus, there were more splendid gladiatorial games and beast hunting shows. Describing the life of those emperors, Julius Capitolinus said that it was an old custom to stage *munera* and *venatio* before emperors went to war. He connects this custom with the need to raise morale amongst Romans heading into battle, and to prepare them for the sights and sounds of war, so that they would be fearless when faced by armed foes or wounds and blood.[55]

Celebrating the millennial anniversary of the founding of Rome in 248, Philip (r. 244–49) put on games using 1,000 pairs of gladiators from Imperial schools, plus a great number of beasts in *venatio*.[56] A man of humour, Gallienus (r. 253–68) celebrated a decade of his rule with truly unforgettable games: the ceremonial procession comprised 1,200 gladiators, splendidly dressed in golden clothes. Once Gallienus sent a laudatory wreath to a 'hunter' who had failed to kill a bull on a dozen occasions. The people expressed surprise to see such a clumsy *venator* awarded, but then Gallienus declared through an announcer: 'It is a difficult thing to miss a bull so many times.'[57]

Celebrating the triumph over the Germans and Blemmyes, Probus (r. 276–82) put on games that included 300 pairs of gladiators, as well as beast baiting. The number of gladiators was comparatively small, but the participation of imprisoned Blemmyes, Germans, Sarmatians and Isaurian robbers provided the games with some distinction.[58]

On the whole, the spectacles shown by Trajan in 107 remained unsurpassed. After his death, the duration of performances as well as the number of gladiators and beasts engaged began to decrease. The only exception was probably the games staged by Commodus — no exact information about them is available, but his passion for gladiatorial combat is well known. There was a certain splash of interest in gladiatorial games under Gordian I and Philip, but other emperors were considerably more modest in terms of entertainment, either for lack of interest or for lack of money.

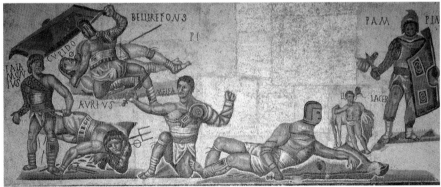

Three fragments of a famous mosaic from Villa Borghese represent gladiatorial combats (between *retiarii* and *secutores*) and a beast hunt (*venatio*). According to the inscriptions all the duels ended in the death of the loser. Early 4th century AD. (Galleria Borghese, Rome / Alinari / The Bridgeman Art Library)

23

Until the mid-1st century BC, gladiatorial fighting generally took place on the Roman Forum (Forum Romanum), as no permanent amphitheatre existed. Spectators sat on specially constructed wooden tribunes. Amphitheatres as special buildings – first wooden, then stone – appeared in the mid-1st century BC. Stone amphitheatres began to be built in significant numbers in the 1st and 2nd centuries AD.

In the Imperial period, gladiatorial games were traditionally held twice a year – in December and March, to mark the end of the year and the beginning of spring. They were also given to celebrate a triumph or the opening of a public building (for example, an amphitheatre), or on other similar public occasions. The funerary aspect of gladiatorial games practically disappeared altogether.

The demise of gladiatorial games is directly connected with the Roman adoption of Christianity. In 313 the Edict of Milan recognized Christianity as a rightful religion, and in 325 Constantine the Great (r. 306–37), the first Roman emperor to embrace Christianity, promoted the new religion by calling the First Ecumenical Council in Nicaea. That same year in Beirut, he made public an edict censuring 'bloody spectacles' and ordering the law courts to send convicts to penal servitude in mines and not to the arena. The edict was really only observed in the eastern provinces of the empire, however. In Italy, Constantine himself disregarded it by granting the priests

Bestiarii in Commodus' underground passage of the Flavian Amphitheatre (Colosseum). The figure on the left is holding a whip in his right hand and a piece of cloth (mappa) in the left. On the right, the figure is teasing an animal using a disc with small bells. The third bestiarius is making an acrobatic jump over a beast. (Vladamir Golubev)

of Umbria and Etruria the right to stage gladiatorial games. This action set a bad example to others, and the games continued, although not at such a grand scale as before. Thus, Calendar of Filocalus states that from 354 gladiatorial games were held only in December, on ten specially indicated days (compared with the 101 days assigned for theatrical performances and 66 for circus shows).[59]

In 357, Emperor Constantius II (r. 337–61) stopped Roman soldiers and officials volunteering for gladiatorial training and fighting in the arena. Eight years later, Emperor Valentinian I (r. 364–75) issued a second edict prohibiting the courts from sentencing criminals 'to the arena'. In 397, the Byzantine Emperor Arcadius (r. 395–408) and the Roman Emperor Honorius (r. 395–423) forbade senators from taking gladiators into service. Finally, in 399, Emperor Honorius closed the remaining gladiatorial schools.[60]

An unforeseen dramatic event truly put an end to the era of gladiatorial games. In the course of a gladiatorial combat on 1 January 404, Telemachus, a Christian monk from Asia Minor, rushed onto the arena in an attempt to separate the fighters. The peacemaker's life came to a deplorable end – a furious mob went for him and tore him to pieces. His martyrdom was not in vain, however – Emperor Honorius prohibited gladiatorial games forever.[61]

BEAST HUNTING – *VENATIO*

The Romans always had a passion for hunting. Many noble Romans, including emperors, were ardent hunters. Famous orators and authors praised the activity for cultivating courage and steadfastness, and those who could bought hunting lands

Bestiarii letting beasts out onto the arena. The date is thought to be AD 20–50. (Museo Archeologico Nazionale, Napoli)

in Gallia and forests in Italy. An enclosure where wild beasts were kept (*leporarium*) for small-scale hunting became a common feature of a rich Roman's country villa. Hunting was regulated by legislation: citizens were only allowed to hunt at a certain distance from towns, and were allowed to hunt all game except lions, which were considered the emperor's property. Hunting on cultivated lands was forbidden.

The term *venatio* (Latin for 'hunting') chiefly referred to an ordinary hunt; later, however, it was applied to a performance involving animals in an amphitheatre or circus. Similarly, the word *venator* (hunter) originally meant an amateur or professional hunter or a slave responsible for *leporarium*, but later referred to a gladiator fighting with a beast in the arena. In the remainder of this book, the words *venatio* and *venator* will be used purely in their gladiatorial context.

Any show that included animals in the arena of an amphitheatre or circus was called *venatio*. *Venatio* included:

A figurine representing a *venatio*. One of the *venatores* has been knocked down, another, protecting himself with a large shield, is probably trying to save him. (Musée Archéologique, Sousse. Author's collection)

- presentations of exotic animals
- entertainment provided by performing animals
- fighting between animals
- hunting animals
- *taurocatapsia* (bull wrestling – see below)
- fighting between animals and *venatores*
- using dangerous animals to execute criminals.

In the Republican period and occasionally later, *venatio* was given in the Great Circus (Circus Maximus). In the Imperial period, however, it became closely connected with *munera* and was moved into the amphitheatre, where *venatio* was part of the morning programme. It was sometimes held in a circus or a stadium.

Venatio was not invariably a bloody entertainment. Exotic animals like giraffes, ostriches or hippopotami were often simply presented to the public for viewing. Some animals were trained to do complicated tricks. Monkeys, for example, were trained to ride on dogs, drive chariots and even act in short theatrical sketches. Responding to a conventional sign, sea lions barked on hearing their names. Elephants were particularly versatile performers, dancing to the music of cymbals struck by other elephants, imitating gladiatorial fights, taking their seats at a banquet table without overturning it, walking along a rope and even drawing Latin and Greek letters. Elephants were reputed to feel a deep sense of responsibility for a show; one story goes that an elephant reprimanded for a poor performance was so upset that he trained through the night all by itself. Sometimes animals dressed in multi-coloured or ludicrous clothes were simply led about the arena. In many ways this part of the spectacle resembled a modern performance in the circus.[62]

For fighting beasts, Romans preferred big and dangerous animals – bears, bulls, lions and the like. Classic pairings were a lion and a tiger, a bull and a bear, a bull and an elephant, an elephant and a rhinoceros, a tiger and a wild boar, and so on. Some mosaics represent more exotic pairs – for example, a bear and a python, a lion and a crocodile, a seal and a bear. Because the animals were sometimes too afraid to fight, they were often chained together to force a clash; elephants were sometimes controlled by a driver, who was unarmed and took no part in fighting. Some events were more a matter of simple baiting than of combat between equal competitors – the outcome of a duel between a lion and a deer was fairly predictable, for example. Dogs, too, occasionally participated in 'hunts', but they more often assisted the *venatores*.

Note that only an armed man fighting with a wild animal was called *venator* – unarmed criminals sentenced to be torn to pieces by beasts were not *venatores* (these unfortunates were known as *damnatus ad bestias*, 'condemned by animal'). Like gladiators, *venatores* were chosen from amongst prisoners of war, slaves, convicts and

Fragment of a famous mosaic from Villa Borghese showing *venatores* fighting with a group of leopards, taken from the early 4th century AD. (Galleria Borghese, Rome / Alinari / The Bridgeman Art Library)

volunteers, and then underwent special training. They stood, however, a grade lower in prestige compared to gladiators, and their salary was lower.

Until recently the term *bestiarius* (from *bestia* — animal, beast) remained ambiguous. It has often been used as a synonym of *venator* or even to refer to all people dealing with animals, including the *damnatus ad bestias*.[63] A detailed examination of iconographic sources, however, makes it difficult to accept either viewpoint and leads us to put *bestiarii* into a separate category. *Bestiarii* were considered even lower in grade than *venatores* and stood on the bottom step of the fighter's hierarchical ladder. They performed multiple roles — animating the performance through acrobatic tricks with dangerous animals, assisting *venatores* by

Two fragments of a relief representing *taurocatapsia*. At the top a rider has caught up with a bull, dropped the reins and caught the bull by the horns. At the bottom, the bull is already lying on the ground and the man is holding him down by the horns. Early 3rd century AD. (Archaeological Museum, Hierapolis. Author's collection)

teasing the animals before the fight (to incite ferocity), catching the attention of animals during combat, as well as giving a hand at the executions of criminals doomed to be torn apart by wild beasts.[64] *Bestiarii* were never armed; they provoked animals with a brightly coloured pieces of cloth (*mappa*), discs with little bells, whips and torches.

Sometimes *taurocatapsia*, which traces its origin back to the famous Cretan bull games, was also included into Roman *venatio*. In this event an acrobat on horseback had to overtake a bull, catch it by the horns, jump onto its back and pull the animal down on the ground. Julius Caesar was the first to show *taurocatapsia* in Rome.[65] Acrobatic *venatores* participating in *taurocatapsia* wore a short, long-sleeved chiton or tunic, tightly fitting knee-length trousers, leather ankle-length shoes, and quilted or leather wraps protecting the belly and chest. Trousers were necessary, as the rider used neither a saddle nor horse-cloth.[66]

The safest pursuit for the *venatores* was straightforward animal hunting against benign creatures such as deer, ostriches and donkeys. The hunts were performed mounted or unmounted, the men being armed with bows and arrows, javelins or

Venatio and *munus* depicted in frescos from Ashik's crypt, Panticapaeum, off the northern coast of the Black Sea. 1st century AD.

hunting spears, and they were meant to demonstrate their skill in using such weapons. Far more dangerous, and therefore amongst the most revered types of *venatio*, was the battle of unmounted *venatores* with wild beasts, such as lions, tigers, leopards or bears. Until the mid-1st century AD, *venatores* in these encounters were

Animals for *venatio*; the name of each animal is indicated: Nilus (the Nile), Alecsandria (Alexandria), Simplicius (Simple), Gloriosus (Glorious) and others. The inscription 'N XVI' on a bull's body shows the number of bulls participating in the venatio. (Musée national du Bardo, Tunis. Author's collection)

equipped like heavily armed gladiators. Later, however, their equipment was lightened and a hunting spear became the only weapon of *venatores* who wore a tunic (see Chapter 2).

A duel between a mounted *venator* and a dangerous beast was even more exotic. Representations of these battles are usually found in the east of the empire, in Asia Minor or north of the Black Sea. In Asia Minor the fighter more often rode a specially trained bull, rather than a horse.[67] North of the Black Sea, the traditions of *munus* and *venatio* were more unique. Bloody games were never widespread here – they were only held in towns housing Roman garrisons or those furnished with a temple dedicated to the cults of Roman emperors. Although the commonest pair of gladiators consisted of a *retiarius* and a *secutor*, the region also had unique types of gladiator that had no analogue in the western parts of the empire (see Chapter 2).

Venator in single combat with a lion. Shown as row of busts, the spectators are in the upper part of the mosaic. The wall of the *podium* can be seen on the right and at the bottom. (Musée national du Bardo, Tunis. Author's collection)

As to *venatio*, frescos from Ashik's crypt in Panticapaeum, the capital of the Bosporan kingdom, show only one combat – one *venator* on foot and five mounted *venatores* fighting deer, boar, bear and leopard or panther. Four out of the five warriors are armed with spears, which are mostly gripped with both hands. The fifth is shooting an arrow at a leopard from a bow. All the horsemen are wearing traditional Bosporan clothes: a knee-length chiton with short sleeves, tightly fitting trousers and leather boots. The *venator* on foot, wearing nothing but a loincloth, is fighting a leopard or panther with a trident.

Some Roman representations occasionally showed children playing the parts of *venatores*. In these rare representations, children are killing hares, cocks or geese with spears or javelins. Such events might have been expressions of aristocratic pride, allowing senators and equestrians to enjoy the 'heroism' of their children in the arena to a standing applause of the public.[68]

The *venator* won his fight against the beast in most encounters. Occasionally an animal gained a victory and was granted its life as a reward. There were beasts that killed a considerable number of *venatores* in the course of their 'career'. The Romans, with a black humour, gave the nickname 'Innocence' to a she-bear repeatedly coming out victorious. *Venatores* could also count upon *missio* (maintaining of life) if they won. A gravely wounded or completely exhausted fighter could ask to quit the arena. However, if his request was refused he had to fight with the next animal.

Many animals, especially famous ones, had personal names, such as *Victor*, *Crudelis* (Crude) and *Omicida* (Killer). An inscription – for example, *n*[umero] *XVI* – is sometimes seen on the body of a bull; it relates the number of bulls taking part in a given performance (see picture on page 30).

On occasions an animal provoked such respect or pity in the spectators that it was saved from death in the arena. The story of Androclus and the lion is a memorable example. Androclus, a slave, escaped to the African desert, where he came across a lion with a thorn in its paw. He pulled out the thorn and the grateful lion remembered the man. Androclus was finally caught and sentenced to be torn to bits by beasts in the Great Circus. Here, at *venatio*, he met that very lion, which recognized the man and refused to attack him. To general surprise, Emperor Augustus called for Androclus and demanded explanation. The latter told the emperor about his first meeting with the lion. Not only did the emperor set Androclus free, but also made him a present of the lion, an act that threw the amphitheatre into joyous applause. Later Androclus earned his living by taking his domesticated lion from one tavern to another and telling his story.[69]

On account of their intelligence and human-like behaviour, elephants aroused more pity than any other animals. Forced to fight with men at a splendid *venatio* showed by Pompey, they faced the challenge at first, but realizing that their position was hopeless, they bent down as if in supplication and seemed to cry for mercy. The spectators were moved to tears and cursed the organizer of the games, vocally forgetting his generosity.[70]

As already noted, animals also delivered executions in the arena. There were several ways to kill criminals condemned to death (*noxii*). During the time of the empire, the executions were often based on a mythological story, resulting in performances

Execution of convicts by wild animals. Tied up with ropes, men are being pushed to the beasts by *bestiarii* who look to have been protecting themselves with spears lying about everywhere. Mosaic dating from the 2nd century AD. (El Djem Museum, Tunisia. Author's collection)

that were grotesque and horrifying in their perversions.[71] For example, the myth of Prometheus was used as the model for executing one Laureolus, accused of either patricide, murdering his patron, the theft of gold from a temple or an intention to set Rome on fire (the author of the relevant primary source could not remember the specific crime). The myth says that Prometheus, charged with stealing the sacred fire from Olympus, was chained to a rock where every day an eagle picked at his liver, the damaged organ being restored again during the night for fresh mutilation the next day. Laureolus was tied to a cross in the arena of the Colosseum and a bear was brought out to deliver the execution.[72] Another convict represented Orpheus, a famous poet and musician from Greek mythology who played his cithern and sang so skilfully that he subjugated not only people and gods but nature itself. The myth was portrayed down to the smallest detail – there were herds of animals and flocks of birds and even 'crawling rocks'. The only thing that differed from the myth was that the bear was not charmed by his singing, and killed the wretch.[73]

To be consigned to *damnatus ad bestias* was considered the cruellest of capital punishments, on a par with being crucified or burnt at the stake. Wearing only loincloths, unarmed and often tied up, the condemned were displayed in the arena, destined to be torn to pieces by hungry beasts. They were sometimes tied to a pole, which was either dug into the ground or fixed on a cart. Some reproductions show the condemned carrying small inscribed tablets, probably describing their crimes. Tied in pairs by the *noxii*, neck, were led into the arena by *bestiarii*, who then set the animals on them. The bodies of the executed *noxii* were usually thrown into the Tiber or another river. However, a burial site containing numerous remains of maimed and dismembered bodies has recently been found in the amphitheatre of Trier, and is widely believed to contain *noxii*.

Roman law, like ancient law in general, determined punishments based not only on the crime committed, but also from the judicial status of the accused. Some particularly egregious or cruel capital punishments (as, for example, being torn apart by beasts or crucified) could not be applied to Roman citizens. The apostles Peter and Paul, for example, were accused of the same crime. The first was sentenced to crucifixion while the second – a Roman citizen – to decapitation.

Execution by means of animals was criticized by some historians and biographers belonging to the senatorial class, ironically both for being too cruel and too gentle. For example, Suetonius criticized Nero for ordering 'that none should be slain, not even the condemned criminals employed in the combats' at the games that Nero gave in the amphitheatre on the Campus Martius. At the same time,

Suetonius attacked Nero for making 'four hundred senators, and six hundred Roman knights, amongst whom were some of unbroken fortune and unblemished reputation, to act as gladiators.'[74] He also blamed Caligula for being too cruel, particularly to the citizens of the 'first estates' (the upper classes),[75] ignoring their

Diptych representing a *venatio*. A diptych is a hinged folding tablet with waxed inner sides used in ancient times for writing on. Later a diptych was made of ivory, gold or silver, richly adorned with relief or carving. A lattice revolving structure (*cochleae*) can be seen on the right hand at the bottom of this example which dates from AD 506. (Schweizerisches Landesmuseum, Zurich)

privileges and subjecting them to punishments meant for the lower classes. The Roman people in general often seem to have disapproved of executions by animals. For example, as a child Emperor Caracalla (r. 211–17) cried and turned away every time he saw the condemned given to the animals, and consequently enjoyed the sympathies of the people for his compassion.[76]

The general Lucius Aemilius Paulus was the first to make animals serve as executioners, when in 167 BC he condemned deserters to be trampled to death by elephants. In 146 BC, Publius Cornelius Scipio the Younger followed his example at his triumph following the seizure of Carthage.[77] The Roman authorities appreciated this form of execution and it was soon one of many accepted punishments in Roman criminal law.

Many of those condemned to execution by beasts were Christians. Before the execution, every effort was made to persuade them to renounce their faith and swear allegiance to the emperor, but this about-turn was unacceptable to most of them. They knew only one God – 'king of kings and emperor of all people.' Yet the late Imperial period saw the disappearance of capital punishment through hanging, crucifixion and wild animal. Of the cruellest executions, only burning at the stake remained.

Venationes were often voluptuously furnished and decorated. Artificial landscapes of rocky hills, trees and water reservoirs attempted to recreate the animals' natural environments on the arena floor. Shows turned into theatrical performances with animals, *venatores* or *noxii* appearing quite unexpectedly, often right in the middle of the arena, where they were delivered from beneath with the help of a complex system of elevators. The first *venatio* took place in Rome in 186 BC. According to Livy, at the games given by Marcus Fulvius to celebrate the victory in the Aetolian War, 'many actors from Greece came to do him honour, and athletic contests were witnessed for the first time in Rome. The hunting of lions and panthers formed a novel feature, and the whole spectacle presented almost as much splendour and variety as those of the present day.'[78] The citizens enjoyed such entertainment and it laid down cultural roots. True, the Senate, cautious either about endangering people or about giving an additional source of income to Carthage, tried to forbid the importation of beasts from Africa to Italy, but the ban was lifted in 170 BC.[79] Already in 169 BC, only 17 years after the first show, 63 leopards, 40 bears and even elephants fought in the arena.[80]

In the 1st century BC, *venatio* was a common entertainment and an indispensable part of the programme of every large gladiatorial games. The number of participating animals grew constantly. In 93 BC, Sulla used 100 lions, while in 58 BC the public enjoyed the fighting of 150 beasts of different kinds, including such exotic animals as crocodiles and hippopotami. (A special pool was dug out for them, probably in the Circus Maximus.[81]) Opening his theatre in 55 BC, Pompey brought out rare Ethiopian rhinoceroses, elephants, wolves and monkeys to stage a particularly luxurious *venatio*. At the games in honour of his triumph in 46 BC, Julius Caesar showed the Romans a giraffe and fought 400 lions in the arena. In addition, bulls were made to fight with horses.

Venatio was a favourite entertainment of many emperors. Augustus prided himself on giving 26 *venationes* during his lifetime, which cost the lives of around 3,500 wild animals, about 135 animals at each show.[82] Caligula and Claudius actually preferred to throw people to the beasts.[83] Claudius was indeed a great admirer of various kinds of *venatio*.[84] Apart from chariot races and Trojan games

This mosaic showing a *venatio* was created on the order of Magerius to commemorate games he had held. Magerius himself can be seen here together with two deities and four *venatores* of the Telegenii Corporation; a servant is holding a tray with four small bags each containing 1,000 sesterces, which were awards for the victorious *venatores*. 3rd century AD. (Musée Archéologique, Sousse. Author's collection)

(competitive games based on horse-riding exercises), he entertained the Circus Maximus with *taurocatapsia* and even African hunting with a detachment of praetorian riders led by tribunes and the prefect (both high-level Roman officials). Claudius sometimes broke off chariot races after every five rounds to show *venatio* (there were usually ten rounds a day, but Claudius raised the number to 24).[85] Commodus was fond *of venatio* too, but his preference, as we have seen, was to kill animals himself.[86] Most frequently, he killed them with arrows from a bow or throwing javelins; he stood on a special platform, thus demonstrating his marksmanship rather than courage. He was an excellent archer – not a single arrow missed the target and every hit was mortal; crescent-shaped arrowheads cut the heads off ostriches that were running at full speed. The Roman people generally disapproved of this cruel entertainment and marvelled only at his deftness.[87] Gratian (r. 367–83) also adored killing animals with arrows.[88]

The number of the animals brought into the arena occasionally reached astronomic figures. For example, during the first 100 days of games given by Emperor Titus in AD 80 to celebrate the opening of the Colosseum, 5,000 various animals were killed. In total, 9,000 animals were slain in *venatio* in the course of the entire games. Even women (possibly volunteers, not specially trained *venatores*) took part in the hunt. Moreover, horses, bulls and other animals were trained to function in shallow water, performing in the water-filled amphitheatre (evidently the water was not very deep, about 1m/3ft 3in. perhaps).[89]

On seizing Jerusalem in 70, even before he became emperor, Titus put on grandiose games to celebrate his brother's birthday. They resulted in the deaths of 2,500 imprisoned Jews, who were forced to fight with wild animals or participate in team combats, although some of the prisoners were simply burnt to death.[90] Hadrian (r. 117–38) gave *venatio* a more international coverage in games shown in various towns across the empire. Thousands of beasts were engaged in a *venatio* in the Athenian stadium: 'In the Circus he had many wild beasts killed and often a whole hundred of lions.'[91] Antoninus Pius (r. 138–61) focused particularly on variety of creatures in his *venationes*: 'He held games, at which he displayed elephants and the animals called corocottae [possibly hyenas] and tigers and rhinoceroses, even crocodiles and hippopotami, in short, all the animals of the whole earth; and he presented at a single performance as many as a hundred lions together with tigers.'[92] Both descriptions show that lion was a comparatively rare and expensive animal at that time.

Gordian I (r. 238) released 100 Libyan beasts of prey into the arena one day and 1,000 bears on another.[93] Judging by the fact that the number of animals was mentioned in his biography, it was doubtless an act of rare generosity. Celebrating his aforementioned triumph over the Germans and Blemmyes, Probus (r. 276–282):

> …gave in the Circus a most magnificent wild beast hunt, at which all things were to be the spoils of the people … through all the entrances were brought in one thousand ostriches, one thousand stags and one thousand wild boars, then deer, ibexes, wild sheep, and other grass-eating beasts, as many as could be reared or captured. The populace was then let in, and each man seized what he wished. Another day he brought out in the Amphitheatre at a single performance one hundred maned lions, which woke the thunder with their roaring. All of these were slaughtered as they came out of the doors of their dens, and being killed in this way they afforded no great spectacle. For there was none of that rush on the part of the beasts which takes place when they are let loose from cages. Besides, many, unwilling to charge, were despatched with arrows. Then he brought out one hundred leopards from Libya, then one hundred from Syria, then one hundred lionesses and at the same time three hundred bears; all of which beasts, it is clear, made a spectacle more vast than enjoyable.[94]

The description shows that the jaded Roman public was hard to shock, least of all by a common slaughter of animals with arrows and javelins. It craved instead for dangerous single combat between man and beast.

Even emperors who disliked *venatio* considered such shows conducive to their popularity and an occasion to demonstrate their generosity. Thus, Marcus Aurelius watched these spectacles unwillingly but 'was so liberal as to present a hundred lions together in one performance and have them all killed with arrows.'[95] He had a habit of reading or listening to reports or writing resolutions during a performance, which often made him the object of ridicule in the eyes of the people.[96] Such behaviour must have been considered extremely impolite. In contrast, Emperor Augustus always apologized when he had to leave the show on business, and appointed a master of ceremonies as a substitute for him, but never did he busy himself with anything unconnected with the arena when he was present.[97]

Later in the ancient period and in the early Middle Ages, the essence of *venatio* changed. What had essentially been a splendidly decorated slaughterhouse on the arena floor gave way to performances in which acrobatic displays occupied an ever-growing part of the programme. We still see images of a *venator* piercing a wild animal with his spear, but *bestiarii* with whips or lassos, various rings or discs are found much more frequently (rings and discs were thrown in different directions to divert the animals' attention). A great admirer of acrobatic and comical tricks, Carus (r. 282–83) was possibly the first to stage this kind of spectacle. Among the tricks he showed were bears 'acting' in a play, a dancer working on the rope, who seemed to fly in the air, and a wall-walker, who teased a bear and then ran away from it.[98]

Comical performances and acrobatic tricks using animals became particularly widespread in the 5th and 6th centuries. Also popular were various devices that helped the 'hunters' to escape from animals. One such device was a lattice revolving structure (*cochleae*) with four panels, behind which a kneeling man could hide from the beast. Another shelter looked like an oval or round cage made of reeds and called a *ericius* (hedgehog), as the man acted like a hedgehog in its classic defensive ball. Another structure was a vertical pole with two baskets, to which people were tied with ropes. The baskets rotated and at the same time moved up and down, which vexed the animals and amused the public. A similar system was attached to a wheel that could not only rotate, but also elevate – a man holding on to the wheel taunted the beasts while himself staying out of danger. Another common trick was performed by acrobats who, with the help of poles, vaulted over the animals, trying to steer clear of their teeth and claws. Having infuriated the beasts, the men then

This diptych of Flavius Anastasius, Roman Consul in 517, illustrates a circus scene with men catching lions with ropes. Two lattice revolving structres can also be seen here. (akg-images / Erich Lessing)

hid themselves behind the doors of the arena. This show demanded exceptional deftness and speed, as the number of doors was insufficient to shelter all the men at the same time.[99]

The formal end to *venatio* came as late as 681, more than two and a half centuries after gladiatorial games were stopped. The last *venatio* took place in the Colosseum in 523, and Theodoric the Great, king of the Ostrogoths, ruler of Italy and regent of the Visigoths, with great reluctance allowed the consul to carry out the performance, expressing his regret over this kind of entertainment.[100]

NAVAL BATTLES – *NAUMACHIA*

Naumachia was a curious form of naval battle that in many ways resembled gladiatorial games. Because of its large scale, a full-sized *naumachia* was typically not held in an arena. Some amphitheatres, however, were furnished with large floor areas specially constructed to allow their filling with water. Even small ships managed to manoeuvre in these pools. Back in AD 57 the arena of a wooden amphitheatre, built on Nero's order on the Campus Martius, was filled with water and various sea animals swam in it. A naval battle between the 'Persians' and the 'Athenians' was then enacted in the pool, before it was drained and a land combat began between two detachments of gladiators was fought.[101] Domitian staged a naval battle in the arena of the Colosseum.[102] It was, however, only a weak copy of *naumachia* – a real *naumachia* would involve dozens of full-size ships carrying thousands of oarsmen and warriors.

The origins of *naumachia* are attributed to Julius Caesar, who put on immense gladiatorial games and theatrical performances when he ruled in Rome during the 1st century BC. According to Suetonius:

> a lake having been dug in the little Codeta, ships of the Tyrian and Egyptian fleets, containing two, three, and four banks of oars, with a number of men on board, afforded an animated representation of a sea-fight. To these various diversions there flocked such crowds of spectators from all parts, that most of the strangers were obliged to lodge in tents erected in the streets, or along the roads near the city. Several in the throng were squeezed to death, amongst whom were two senators.[103]

A total of 2,000 oarsmen and 1,000 warriors were engaged in this clash, shown in 46 BC. In 43 BC, a year after Caesar's death, the lake was drained for fear that its stagnation would contribute to the spread of a raging epidemic.

Naumachiae were mostly held on artificial lakes in Rome. The biggest complex was built in the southern part of the modern district of Trastevere. In the middle of an elliptically shaped lake measuring 548×365m, there was an artificial island 100m in diameter. The lake was large enough for real warships, though not the biggest types, to manoeuvre. In 2 BC, Augustus showed an imitation of the battle of Salamis (480 BC) here, with 30 triremes and biremes supplied with battering rams, as well as numerous smaller ships taking part in the *naumachia*. Some 3,000 gladiators were engaged, besides oarsmen and sailors.[104]

The lake in Trastevere, made by Emperor Augustus, continued to be used for *naumachia*. It saw impressive games given by Emperor Titus in AD 80 to celebrate the opening of the Colosseum – the games began with a big *naumachia* followed by gladiatorial games and a *venatio*, held on a platform built over the lake during an intermission. On the same day, the flooded Colosseum accommodated small ships playing out a battle between the Corcyreans and the Corinthians in a mini *naumachia*. The second day was assigned to horse racing and the third to *naumachia* again. This battle between the 'Athenians' and 'Syracusans' involved 300 men. The 'Athenians' overcame the enemy: not only did they gain victory 'at sea', but they also landed on a tiny island and seized its fortress.[105]

The greatest *naumachia* was given by Claudius on the natural Fucine Lake, not far from Rome, in 52.[106] The ships carried over 19,000 prisoners, of whom some represented the Sicilians, others the Rhodians. This is how Tacitus described the battle:

Claudius equipped triremes and quadriremes with nineteen thousand men; he lined the circumference of the lake with rafts, lest there were some means of escape at various points, but he still left full space for the strength of the crews, the skill of the pilots, the impact of the vessels, and the usual operations of a naval battle. Companies of the praetorian cohorts and cavalry stood on the raft, with a breastwork in front of them, from which catapults and ballistas were to be worked. The rest of the lake was occupied by marines on decked vessels. Crowds of people from the neighbouring towns, others from Rome itself, eager to see the sight or to show respect to the emperor, covered the banks, the hills, and mountain tops, which thus resembled a theatre. The emperor presided, with Agrippina seated near him; he had a splendid military cloak on, she wore a mantle of cloth of gold. A battle was fought courageously by brave men, though it was between condemned criminals. After much bloodshed they were released from the necessity of mutual slaughter.[107]

The command to begin fighting was given by a silver Triton, a Greek sea-god, half-man, half-dolphin, emerging from the water. It was in the course of the performance that the condemned prisoners spoke the famous words: 'Ave Caesar, morituri te salutant' ('Hail, Caesar, those who are about to die salute you').[108] By contrast, there is no evidence of gladiators speaking these words in the arena of an amphitheatre.

Under Domitian (r. 81–96), a new lake was made for *naumachia* near the Tiber. In a large-scale *naumachia* performed here in 89, a heavy shower contributed to the death of nearly all the participants and many spectators, who caught some form of illness.[109] Trajan (r. 98–117) made another lake for *naumachia* (the *naumachia Vaticana*), located to the north-west of the Mausoleum of Hadrian (now Castle Sant'Angelo) erected later in Rome.[110] However, not a single description of a *naumachia* given by Emperor Trajan has been found. By contrast, the corrupt and excessive Elagabalus gave *naumachia* in the Circus, in canals filled with wine.[111] In 248, Emperor Philip celebrated a *naumachia* in honour of the anniversary of the city of Rome.[112] The last time that *naumachia* is mentioned among other spectacles (theatrical performances, circus games, *venatio* and gladiatorial games), it refers to an event shown by Aurelian in 274.[113]

Prisoners and condemned criminals made up the bulk of the fighters in *naumachia*, but specially trained gladiators also participated. All the fighters were called *naumachiarii* or *naumachi*. The Romans were especially keen on reconstructing historical battles in *naumachia*; the outcome, however, was often at variance with reality. Thus, in the above mentioned 'battle of Salamis', given by Augustus, the 'Greeks' defeated the 'Persians' as had really occurred, but the 'battle of Syracuse' held under Titus brought victory to 'Athenians', who lost the real naval battle that took place in 424 BC. Because the Romans were reluctant to see their army defeated even in a play, the historical subjects for *naumachia* were chosen from the war histories of Greece or the Near East; battles involving Roman troops were never staged.

Naumachiae were the most expensive of all performances. They required artificial lakes to be made, warships brought over and thousands of men taught the skills of naval warfare. Therefore, *naumachiae* were held far less frequently than gladiatorial games and their organization was the emperors' prerogative.

CHAPTER II

THE TYPES OF GLADIATOR

Accurately classifying gladiators and their equipment at the time of the early Republic is extremely challenging due to the lack of almost any sources – iconographic, written or archaeological. The frescos found in the archaeological excavations of Paestum, dating back to the 4th century BC, supposedly reveal the earliest image of gladiators. Armed with spears, they are shown fighting in pairs. Some are wearing tunics, others only loincloths. Their heads are protected with splendid bronze helmets in the southern Greek-Italian fashion common at the time, and each gladiators carries a large, round, curved shield that strongly resemble *aspis*, the shields used by Greek hoplites.

After the 4th century BC, the tradition of depicting combat ceases. Weapons are rarely found, as with the growth of Roman influence the tradition of burying weapons in tombs also died away. Therefore, the 3rd and 2nd centuries BC offer practically no iconographic artefacts and archaeological finds are scarce. Only the end of the Republic period brings more information about gladiators. A whole series of tomb reliefs has been found in various locations, dating back to the 1st century BC and depicting gladiatorial combat. Most of the gladiators are wearing nothing but a *subligaculum* loincloth with a *balteus* sword belt. The legs of many of the men are protected with *ocreae* (greaves).

Our knowledge of the types of gladiators and their equipment comes chiefly from sources dating from the 1st–3rd centuries AD. It was Octavian Augustus (r. 27 BC–AD 14) who shaped the institution of the gladiators into a clear-cut structure.

Therefore, the description of the types of gladiators and their equipment given below generally reflects the state of things in the Imperial period, which is replete with sources, although some characteristics of earlier equipment, where information is available, will also be explained. Moreover, traditional types of gladiators and gladiatorial equipment had reached a stable state in the western parts of the empire by *c.* 100, and remained practically unchanged until the end of the gladiatorial era, whereas the eastern empire searched for new types of gladiatorial equipment throughout the period. The resulting differences will be considered. Our reconstruction of the gladiators' appearance will begin with the main categories of gladiator (at least those of which a sufficient amount of information is available). Other types will then be examined on the basis of the scraps of knowledge we have.

ARBELAS

Some iconographic sources from the eastern Roman Empire reveal a particular type of gladiator, called *scissor* by Junkelmann.[114] Yet the term *scissor* is only mentioned once in the list of gladiators of the *lanista* C. Salvius Capito. (A *lanista* was a private entrepreneur preparing gladiators in a gladiatorial school and then lending or selling them to an *editor*.) Here a *scissor* is mentioned along with *eques,*

A duel between a *retiarius* and an *arbelas* (right), dating from around the 2nd–3rd century AD. (Author's reconstruction, artist Vladimir Golubev)

Two *arbelases* in combat depicted in two fragments of the same relief. The right-hand combatant in the bottom relief has lost his weapon and the left-hand fighter is transferring the combat onto the ground. It dates from the early 3rd century AD. (Archaeological Museum, Hierapolis. Author's collection)

thraex, myrmillo, retiarius, sagittarius, veles, hoplomachus, samnis and *gallus*.[115] This evidence belongs to the Republic period, and probably to the 1st century BC. *Scissor* is not to be found later, which suggests that this type of gladiator had either disappeared or changed its name. In favour of the latter possibility is the mention of a gladiator called *arbelas* (Greek αρβηλας)[116] in Artemidorus' *Oneirocritica (The Interpretation of Dreams)*, written in the 2nd century AD. Here an *arbelas* is equated with a *dimachaerus* (see below) and the author judges both of them as the craftiest fighters in the arena. The word *arbelas* probably comes from a semi-circular shoemaker's knife (Greek αρβηλος) that closely resembled the weapon used by this gladiator. It is likely that this type of gladiator was first named *scissor* and then renamed *arbelas*.

An *arbelas* is standing on the right-hand side of this relief. The figure on the left does not survive, but judging by the similar shape of the opponents' helmet it was also an *arbelas*. Early 3rd century AD. (Archaeological Museum, Hierapolis. Author's collection)

Today there are six known images of an *arbelas*. Three of them represent *arbelases* without adversaries, one shows a *retiarius* fighting with an *arbelas*, and the other two seem to depict combat between two *arbelases*. So we can at least conclude that an *arbelas* could fight with a *retiarius* or another *arbelas*. The armour is undoubtedly made of scales in two reliefs and possibly of mail in the others – the dress is hardly likely to be a simple tunic, as in this case the fighting would end too quickly when someone landed the first blow.[117] Furthermore, gladiators of the same type would hardly wear armour on one occasion and nothing but a tunic on another.

So the *arbelas* is equipped with a helmet, scale armour or mail covering his body almost to the knees, a quilted or metal laminar *manica* armguard on his right arm,[118] and short greaves on both legs. (A greave usually reaches to the knee, but in a relief from Bodrum they are quite short and only cover half of the shin.) The reliefs also show closed helmets fitted with visors. Two helmets have a crest, like a *secutor*'s helmet (an *arbelas* may have received such a helmet when fighting with a *retiarius*). Helmets with a smooth surface, including those worn by *arbelases* fighting with each other, are represented in three reliefs. In one of the reliefs the shape of the helmet is unclear. An *arbelas* carried no shield, but is seen holding an unusual weapon in his left hand; the weapon has a tubular vambrace (armoured forearm piece) ending in a crescent-shaped blade. It was probably effective in cutting through a net or warding off a *retiarius*' trident. In his right hand an *arbelas* held a dagger, which has

a straight blade in most reliefs. It seems to be curved and looks like a *sica* in the relief from Bodrum; this relief is damaged, however, so we cannot be sure of the shape of that particular dagger.

The unusual weapon held in the left hand must have inflicted horrible lacerations. It was probably sharpened along both the outer and inner surfaces of the blade, so it could cut on the thrust as well as the withdrawal (the latter is clearly seen in one of the reliefs where a gladiator is about to cut off his opponent's head, while the latter is doing his best to obstruct him with his hands). The weapon may have been imperfect because of a flimsy fixation of the tubular vambrace – in both reliefs depicting *arbelases* in combat the vambrace lies on the ground at the end of the fighting. As not a single surviving example of this weapon has been found, one can only guess at the position of the handle or whether the vambrace was fastened on the hand. A perpendicular grip similar to that of the Indian *katar* or *pata* seems to be likely for such a weapon. In this case, however, it would have been fixed firmly enough. Maybe the vambrace was sometimes thrown down on purpose, when entering close combat. With the total equipment probably weighing 22–26kg, an *arbelas* was the most heavily armed of all the gladiators.

VENATOR

The *venator*, as we have seen, was a beast fighter, assisted by a *bestiarius*. Strictly speaking, *venatores* were not proper gladiators: they took part in *venatio*, but not in *munera*. *Venatores* were a step lower in rank than gladiators, yet it is most appropriate to examine *venatores*' equipment alongside the other types of fighter.

Up to the mid-1st century AD, reliefs depict the *venatores*' equipment as similar to that of heavily armed gladiators: they wore loincloths or tunics, helmets, leg-wrappings and often greaves, and the short *manica* armguard; they also carried large shields and swords or spears. The shields were square, as a rule, but could also be round or oval. Even a *venator* dressed in scale armour can be seen in one of the reliefs. There is an opinion that it is gladiators, not *venatores*, who are fighting with beasts in these reliefs.[119] If so, it means that until the mid-1st century AD heavily armed gladiators sometimes fought with wild beasts in a type of disorderly carnage, and that various types of gladiators could be involved. In these reliefs we possibly see *equites* (in scale armour and specific helmet), *hoplomachi*, *myrmillones* and *thracians* (recognizable by their shields and helmets).

Relief showing a *venatio* fighting with a bear and lions in front of spectators. The *venetars* are equipped differently – holding a round or rectangular shield and straight swords, wearing various helmets, short *manicae* and tunics with an open shoulder or completely closed. 1st century AD. (akg-images / Nimatallah)

An early *venatio* is represented in this relief. There are two types of *venator*, one wearing scale armour and armed with a round shield and a sword (lying in the bottom left-hand corner), others are wearing tunics and can be seen to be armed with rectangular shields and swords. Late 1st century BC. A plaster cast of the original is kept at the Villa Torlonia, Rome. (akg-images / Electa)

Far left: *Venatores* ready to kill different animals are reproduced in these three fragments of a large mosaic from North Africa. There are considerable differences in the *venatores'* equipment. 3rd century AD. (Musée Archéologique, Sousse. Author's collection)

49

Below left:
Three fragments of the mosaic showing a *venatio* held by Magerius. Every *venator* has different equipment: one has only a loincloth on, others are wearing tunics; one has a *manica* on his left arm, others have not. The loops of the *manica* used for fastening the flap protecting the wrist are clearly seen. 3rd century AD. (Musée Archéologique, Sousse. Author's collection)

A *bestiarius* dealing a final blow to a wounded leopard. The stick he is holding looks to be much thinner than the spear that hit the animal. First half of the 3rd century. Detail from the floor mosaic of the Roman villa in Nennig, Saarland. (akg-images)

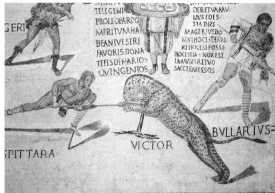

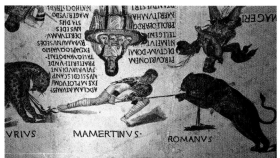

Two heavily armed *venatores* can be seen here with different equipment: one is wearing a tunic and a helmet, armed with a sword and a round shield, while the other is naked except for a loincloth. He has a helmet and is armed with a sword and a large rectangular shield *scutum*. The first *venator*'s left shin appears to be protected with a greave and his thigh with a quilted wrapping. It is a unique type of a *venator*'s equipment. The statues and columns suggest that the *venatio* took place in the Circus Maximus. The relief is from 1st century AD and can be found at the Musée d'Art et d'Histoire, Genève. (akg-images / Bildarchiv Steffens)

A *venatio* probably held in the Circus Maximus. Two *venatores* can be seen in this relief: one is heavily armed (wearing a helmet, holding a shield and a sword) while the other is lightly armed (wearing a tunic and holding a spear). Mid-1st century AD. From the Campana Collection, Museo Nazionale Romano delle Terme. (akg-images / Erich Lessing)

From the mid-1st century AD, heavily armed *venatores* are no longer depicted. Like common hunters, *venatores* now wear only tunics and short knee-length *fasciae* (leg-wrappings) and they carry a hunter's *venabulum* spear as their principal weapon. These lightly armed *venatores* probably existed earlier as well, co-existing with the heavily armed variety (if we admit the latter existed and differed from gladiators).

The 2nd century AD saw *venatores* wearing trousers that reached as far as the knees, plus broad belts and sometimes even small decorated breastplates. In the next century, however, their equipment was again reduced to a tunic. A spear, however, remained their main weapon, and occasionally they seem to have used a shield too. Short leg-wrappings were always a part of their outfit. A *venator* could sometimes be seen wearing a leather or quilted *manica*. This armguard protected his left arm, which was close to the beast — since the spear was rather short, about a man's height in length, and even a beast spitted with a spear could still reach the man with its paws. In a 6th-century relief, a *venator* can be shown with his left arm covered with a *manica* that widened out into a large plate protecting the entire left half of his breast.

In Africa Proconsularis and in the east of the empire, *venatores'* equipment was distinguished by considerable originality. Alongside equipment traditional for the rest of the empire, there were some unique items in a *venator's* wardrobe. For example, in one depiction we can clearly see a leather cuirass consisting of a breastplate and backplate, worn over a *venator's* tunic. Another mosaic shows four *venatores* preparing to kill numerous animals. All the *venatores* are wearing tunics; one is armed with a spear, another with a double-edged sword, a third with a straight but seemingly one-

Fragment of a famous mosaic from Villa Borghese with a *venatio*. There are wounded and dead *venatores* on the left while on the right a few *venatores* are still fighting various beasts (lions, bulls, antelopes, wild boars and ostriches) in this scene from AD 320. (Galleria Borghese, Rome / Alinari / The Bridgeman Art Library)

edged sword (like a cutlass), and the fourth with a sabre (not a curved dagger, but a long blade sabre). The latter is especially curious, as nowhere else is a sabre represented as a gladiator's or *venator's* weapon. The *venatores* are shown preparing for combat: one is getting his sword out of the sheath, the other has already pulled his sword out but not yet thrown off the sheath (there is no shoulder belt or waist belt, so the sheath was undoubtedly thrown off before entering combat).

A *venator's* costume was often very colourful and luxuriously adorned. The short tunic had short or long sleeves, both of which allowed the necessary freedom of movement, and it was frequently trimmed with a fringe, its front and back ornamented with bright embroidery or appliqué. The most common motifs comprised a lion's head or an animal's hide, a star, plus geometrical or abstract figures.

Two *bestiarii* armed with whips are trying to release a comrade from a bear's paws. Note the thick quilted wrappings on the *bestiarii's* left arms. This mosaic is from around the first half of the 3rd century AD. Detail from the floor mosaic of the Roman villa in Nennig, Saarland. (akg-images)

Venatores, 1st century BC.
(Author's reconstruction,
artist Vladimir Golubev)

In contrast to *venatores*, *bestiarii* never carried any weapons, only a whip and a torch, and the *mappa* and bells previously noted. They usually wore loincloths and short tunics and protected their legs with quilted leg-wrappings and their left arms with a thick quilted wrappings. In sources from late antiquity and early Middle Ages, *bestiarii* are occasionally depicted wearing a sort of quilted coat that protected the whole body and even a helmet with numerous little round apertures at the front (similar to modern fencing masks). *Bestiarii* teased beasts with lassos, whips and various metal rings and discs.

HOPLOMACHUS

A *hoplomachus* (or *oplomachus*) was equipped with a helmet, a small round shield, a pair of high greaves and a *manica* on his right arm. He was armed with a spear and a dagger or short sword. A *hoplomachus* fought bare chested. His only clothes, like those of many other types of gladiator, comprised the *subligaculum* loincloth and the *balteus* belt.

The *hoplomachus'* broad-brimmed helmet was supplied with a visor, a crest and a feather on either side, and greatly resembles a *thraex's* helmet. In its shape and

Venator, 3rd–4th centuries AD. (Author's reconstruction, artist Vladimir Golubev)

structure, the *hoplomachus'* bronze shield (*parmula*) looked like a smaller copy of a Greek hoplite's shield. The latter is more widely known under the name of *aspis*, but sometimes is called *hoplon*, explaining the etymology behind the word 'hoplite'. The word *hoplon* is very rarely used in the singular, and its plural *hopla* describes weapons collectively. The name *hoplomachus* is derived from the Greek and means 'fighting with weapons' (*hoplon* – 'weapon', and *machein* – 'to fight'). A *hoplomachus'* weapons – a spear and a short sword – were also similar to those of Greek hoplites. Thus a *hoplomachus* represented a classic heavily armed Greek warrior in the gladiatorial arena.

By the structure of its handle, the *parmula* also resembled a hoplite's shield. It allowed a *hoplomachus* to hold a dagger as a secondary weapon in his left hand and manoeuvre a spear with his right hand. In case the spear was lost, the gladiator put the dagger into his right hand and was able to hold the shield with the left hand using its central handle.

As a *hoplomachus* was only equipped with a small shield, his legs required substantial protection. Covering both the shin and the knee, his greave reached high up to the middle of his thigh. Under the greaves he wore tight, quilted but very soft cloth trousers that covered from his feet to up under his loincloth. The trousers not only covered the unprotected upper parts of the thighs, but also served as a lining for the greave, softening blows and making the high and heavy greaves less uncomfortable. Judging by some frescos, the trousers were often adorned with embroidery. Such greaves and tight quilted trousers were part of the costume of a *thraex*, who also had nothing to defend himself with except a small shield. Indeed, the *hoplomachus'* equipment strongly resembled that of a *thraex*. The difference lay in the offensive weapon, the shape of the shield and the crest of the helmet. Like a *thraex's* armour, the armour of a *hoplomachus* weighed up to 17–18kg, so the *hoplomachus* also falls into the category of heavily armed gladiator.[120]

A *hoplomachus* usually had a *myrmillo* as an adversary, but he is occasionally depicted fighting with a *thraex*. It was probably because he imitated a Greek warrior in the arena that the *hoplomachus* was not recognized as a type of gladiator in eastern parts of the empire (in Greece and its *poleis*). He was, however, widespread in the West. Although a *hoplomachus–myrmillo* pair was less common here than a *myrmillo–thraex* pair, it was still very popular.

A *hoplomachus* fighting with a *myrmillo*, AD 200. (Römermuseum, Augst)

DIMACHAERUS

Written evidence or iconographic artefacts pertaining to this type of gladiator are extremely scarce and often contradictory. A *dimachaerus* certainly fought with two swords or daggers in combat, one in either hand. There seems to be only one relief that undoubtedly depicts a *dimachaerus* – in it a gladiator is armed with two sword-daggers, of which at least one is curved (like the *sica* used by the *thraex*).[121] His head is protected by a broad-brimmed close helmet, his legs covered with greaves. He is either wearing a tunic or mail armour. The latter seems more probable as he would be too vulnerable otherwise, having no shield for protection and only a short weapon for defence. An analogy with the *arbelas* suggests itself: similarly armed, the latter was clad in scale armour or mail.

Below: The only unequivocal reproduction of a *dimachaerus*, early 3rd century AD. (Archaeological Museum, Hierapolis. Author's collection)

Other depictions sometimes attributed to the *dimachaerus* are disputable. One shows a *retiarius* holding two daggers in addition to a trident; another represents a gladiator carrying a shield and two daggers. Based on these artefacts as well as the etymology of *dimachaerus*, some scholars come to the conclusion that the *dimachaerus* did not exist as a distinct type of gladiator; the word was just the name given to gladiators of any type capable of fighting using one or the other hand alternately.[122] However Artemidorus in his *Oneirocritica* mentions a *dimachaerus* alongside a *thraex*, *secutor*, *retiarius*, *essedarius* and *arbelas*.[123] There is also epigraphic evidence to substantiate the existence of this type.[124] If we single out the *arbelas* mentioned only by Artemidorus, as a distinct type of gladiator, why should we refuse this recognition to the *dimachaerus*? Or why should the word διμαχαιρος be understood as 'capable of equally using both hands' instead of 'armed with two blades' (swords, daggers)? I would argue that all these facts together with what we see in the relief allows us to admit the existence of the *dimachaerus* as a distinct type of gladiator. (See reconstruction of the *dimachaerus* on page 132.) Note also that a *dimachaerus* probably had another *dimachaerus* as an opponent.

MYRMILLO

The *myrmillo* gladiator entered the arena about the mid-1st century BC. It is possible that a *gallus* (gladiator), never again mentioned from that time, was renamed *myrmillo* (see below). The name *myrmillo* (also *mirmillo*, *mormillo* or *murmillo*) is frequently associated with the sea fish *mormylos*. Hence the *myrmillo* is

The finale of a combat between a *hoplomachus* and a *myrmillo*. The *myrmillo* has thrown off his shield and raised a finger begging for mercy. (Author's reconstruction, artist Vladimir Golubev)

often confused with the *retiarius'* adversary, the *secutor*. The *myrmillo*, however, appeared about the mid-1st century BC, while the *retiarius* was never heard of until the early Imperial period. This fact allows Junkelmann to suggest that the etymology of the term should not be traced to the name of a sea fish, which implies the existence of a fisherman (*retiarius*), but from the word *murex* (sea snail, spine), which a *myrmillo* may have resembled owing to his helmet or a large shield.[125] There are, however, some rare artefacts in which a fish is clearly seen on a *myrmillo*'s helmet.

The *myrmillo* entered combat with nothing on except the *subligaculum* and the broad *balteus*. His defensive armour comprised a helmet, a *manica* on his right arm, a short greave on his left leg only and a large *scutum*. The helmet had broad brims, a visor and was crowned with a peculiar crest in the shape of a huge fish dorsal fin. The fin was usually decorated with a plume made from feathers or horsehair. Two more feathers were often put on either side of the bowl. The structure of a *myrmillo*'s helmet was very much like that of a *thraex*'s helmet and only differed in the crest. Like other types of gladiators, *myrmillones* had plain polished bronze helmets, but there is an existing helmet that has a unique finishing – it is silvered to resemble fish scales. It must have gleamed wonderfully in the sun on the arena floor.

A greave protected the *myrmillo*'s left leg, but only below the knee. It was worn over thick quilted leg-wrappings made of cloth. The lower part of the greave had a deep U-shaped cut so that it made a smooth adjustment to the thick cloth foot-wrappings. The greave was fastened on the leg by belts attached to two or three pairs of rings fixed onto the greave. A *myrmillo* wore nothing but gaiters on his right leg.

A *myrmillo* protected himself with a 1m-high *scutum* shield. Following the example of Roman legionaries, *myrmillones* were equipped with an oval *scutum* until the mid-1st century AD and later changed it for a rectangular one. The shield covered a gladiator from the greave to the chin. This type of gladiator also fought

A figurine supposedly of a *myrmillo,* 1st–2nd century AD. Note a curious detail about the shield, which is adorned with a picture of fighting gladiators. (British Museum, London. Author's collection)

with an ordinary 40–55cm long *gladius* infantry sword that had a straight, rather broad blade. Being the *myrmillo*'s only weapon, it was often tied to his hand with belts to prevent it being lost in combat. The total weight of a *myrmillo*'s armour reached 16–18kg, with the shield the heaviest item. Thus a *myrmillo* was classified as one of the heavily armed gladiators.

Myrmillones were never engaged in combat with each other. They were generally paired with a gladiator equipped with a small shield – a *thraex* or a *hoplomachus*. A *myrmillo* and a *thraex* was a common pairing and one of the most popular in the Imperial period. They were usually called *scutarii* and *parmularii* after the types of their shields: a *myrmillo* carried the large *scutum* while a *thraex* used a small *parmula*. Marcus Aurelius illustrates their popularity when he thanks his tutor for being uninterested in the outcome of the duels either between the Greens and the Blues or between *parmularii* and *scutarii* (the Greens and the Blues are the teams of supporters at races) – such disinterest was an incredibly rare phenomenon in those days.[126] Domitian preferred a *myrmillo* to any other type of gladiator, and even threw a man to the dogs for speaking out in favour of a *thraex* gladiator.[127]

Relief with two fighting *provocatores*. A slightly damaged inscription says that the left-hand *provocator* belongs to Ludus Julianus, the most famous gladiatorial school, founded by Julius Caesar in Capua. This gladiator has won five combats (including the one pictured here) surpassing all his opponents so brilliantly that he was awarded a laurel wreath, (an exceptional award only given for outstanding prowess displayed in fighting, unlike the palm branch given for every victory). His opponent (the right-hand *provocator*) has lost the combat, which is clear from the fact he has dropped his shield on the ground and is holding up his right arm. The inscription also says that the public pardoned the defeated *provocator* and granted him his life. The wounded *myrmillo* (on the right) also left the arena alive but later died from the received injuries. 30–10 BC. (Topfoto / Werner Forman)

PROVOCATOR

The *provocator* appeared during the late Republic period and remained throughout the Imperial period. There is an argument that this type of gladiator was originally a criminal or prisoner of war sentenced to capital punishment, who could, however, obtain mercy by winning the sympathies of the spectators.[128] Such is suggested by the term *provocator*, which derives from a Roman judicial term at the time of the Republic: it said that a condemned prisoner had the right of appeal to the people (*provocatio ad populum*). A *provocator's* way of fighting, involving false retreats followed by lightning counterattacks, changed the implication and meaning of the term, however.

This gladiator wore a *subligaculum*, a broad metal *balteus*, a *manica* on his right arm, a knee-high greave on his left leg, a breastplate and a helmet; he was equipped with a large rectangular shield and a sword with a straight blade. The large *cardiophylax* metal plate protecting his chest was a characteristic feature of a *provocator*. More often than not it was rectangular in shape, but in the later period crescent-shaped breastplates were also used. The plate appears to have been all metal, as a rule, although some exceptions are known. For example, in the group of *provocatores* in the centre of a monument from Pompeii, the victor has turned his front to the spectators and it can be seen that his breastplate consists of scales and is adorned with a relief showing the Gorgon's head. The plate was fastened with leather belts fastened in a cruciform pattern at the back.

At the turn of ears, *provocatores'* helmets hardly differed from those worn in the Roman Army; moreover, gladiators received the latest model, which had only just begun to gain in popularity among legionaries. In time the helmet changed in format: the cheek-guards disappeared and a visor with round, lattice apertures for eyes appeared instead; the neck-guard constantly increased in size to cover the neck on the sides as well as on the back. Later helmets had broad brims bent down and protecting the whole of the neck. A *provocator's* helmet usually lacked a crest or the plume.[129] It was occasionally adorned with two feathers, stuck on either side of the helmet bowl.

A *provocator* surrounded with wreaths won in the course of his career, 3rd century AD. His armament is that of a later type of *provocator*: a crescent-shaped breastplate, a helmet with broad brims bent downward to protect the neck. (Antikensammlung, Staatliche Muzeen zu Berlin. Author's collection)

A *provocator's* shield looked like a *myrmillo's scutum* on the whole, but it may have been smaller in size, as his greave reached higher than a *myrmillo's* greaves. Earlier the shields were oval; later they became rectangular with slightly sharpened top and bottom edges. *Provocatores'* shields lacked a characteristic oval boss (*umbo*) as a rule; they had only a vertical *spina* rib.

The total weight of *provocator's* armour reached 14–15kg, so he was classified as a medium-armed gladiator. In combat a *provocator* was only matched with another *provocator*; he almost never opposed a gladiator of any other type. There is only one inscription naming a *myrmillo* as a *provocator's* adversary.[130]

RETIARIUS

The *retiarius* (from *rete* – 'net') is the most easily identified type of gladiator. A *retiarius* carried no shield, he wore neither helmet nor greaves; a *manica* protected his left arm, not his right arm as was in case with gladiators of all the other types. He fought with a net, a trident and a dagger. A characteristic feature of a *retiarius* was the *galerus*, a metal shoulder-guard fastened to the *manica*. It is easy to make out a *retiarius* in a group of gladiators by these distinguishing features. The only type that can be confused with a *retiarius* is a *laquearius*, of which very little is known except for the fact that he was equipped like a *retiarius* but was probably armed with a lasso and a spear.

The *retiarius* appeared in the arena as late as the early Imperial period. Until the beginning of this era neither the *retiarius* nor the *secutor*, his adversary, is depicted in a single large panoramic relief representing gladiators. The *retiarius–secutor* pair provided some of the best-loved gladiatorial combats. It gained popularity in the mid-1st century AD and kept its appeal until gladiatorial games were abolished.

A *retiarius* is usually shown wearing nothing but a *subligaculum*; occasionally, however, he is wearing a light tunic open at his right shoulder. His left hand, which held the net, was protected by a *manica*. The *galerus* shoulder protection was fastened on the upper part of the *manica*. The *galerus* was a 1.1–1.2kg heavy bronze plate, almost square, with the side about 30–35cm long. It had two pairs of loops on its inner side so that it could be fastened on the arm. Apparently the belt sometimes ran diagonally across the chest and back and was done up under the right armpit; however, no such belt can be seen in most reliefs, which leads us to the conclusion that it was only fastened on the left arm, as a rule. The *galerus* projected about 12–13cm above the shoulder, protecting the neck and most of the head from lateral blows. The upper edge of the shoulder-guard was slightly bent outward, which retarded sliding blows and allowed the head to move easily. In later times (the 2nd–3rd centuries), a *retiarius* sometimes fought without a *galerus*, at least in the east of the empire. Instead of a shoulder-guard, his left arm, the shoulder and a part of his chest were covered with a metal (scale or mail) *manica*.

Shoulder-guard *galerus* from the gladiatorial school in Pompeii. It is decorated with a medallion with Hercules' image. 1st century AD. (Museo Archeologico Nazionale, Napoli)

A *fuscina* (trident) was the main weapon of a *retiarius*. Having successfully thrown a net over his opponent, a *retiarius* had made only one step on his way to victory. Mostly, however, the *retiarius* seems to have missed his target on the first attempt, and then the *secutor* would try his best to prevent him from picking up the net. Sooner or later a *retiarius* was left with just a trident and a dagger – now he could either hold the trident with both hands or leave it in his right hand, taking the dagger with the left. The first option was preferable, as it was equally hard and ineffective to handle a heavy trident with

Above: A bronze figurine of a *retiarius*, 1st–2nd centuries AD. (British Museum, London. Author's collection)

Below: Combat between a *retiarius* and a *secutor* pictured on a jug. The *retiarius* is preparing to throw a net over his opponent. 2nd century AD. (Historisches Museum der Pfalz, Speyer)

only one arm and use a dagger to parry blows struck with a sword. When fighting on foot, holding a shaft weapon with both hands was preferable, as it allowed the combatant to use both ends of the weapon in parrying and striking blows. The blows themselves were heavier and more effective with the two-handed grip. The lethality of such blows is a strong reason why the *secutor*'s helmet had a smooth surface: it increased the possibility of a heavy thrust sliding along the surface without doing harm to the head. A trident also allowed the *retiarius* to catch the adversary's blade between the points of the weapon or to press the edges of the shield. Blows dealt to the opponent's legs were no less dangerous. Although the *secutor*'s left leg was protected with a greave, he could be knocked down when his left leg was attacked with a trident. The length of a trident approximately equalled a man's height.

It is important to note that the net cannot always be seen in the representations of *retiarii*. Numerous explanations have been advanced in an attempt to explain this problem. The simplest is that the *retiarius* has thrown his net unsuccessfully, missed the target and lost the net. However, a shield lost by a combatant can often be seen lying at his feet. If a lost shield is worth depicting, why not a lost net? It is possible that, finding it difficult to represent a net, the artists simply omitted it, as they are known to have swapped a sword and a shield in the combatant's hands or even deprived him of one of them just for the sake of making a picture clearer. Also surprising is the fact that the images of a *retiarius* covering his adversary with a net are very scarce – this is an impressive moment in the combat, and easily represented.

There is a depiction on a jug, however, showing a *retiarius* about to throw a net upon the adversary. (See picture on the left.) His right hand, clutching a net, is drawn back ready for a throw. He is holding a trident and a dagger in his left hand, the former with its points turned down lest they should catch on the flying net. This depiction, however, can't support the conclusion that the net was always thrown with the right hand. The artist probably swapped the weapons in the *retiarius*' hands, a fairly common technique in other depictions of

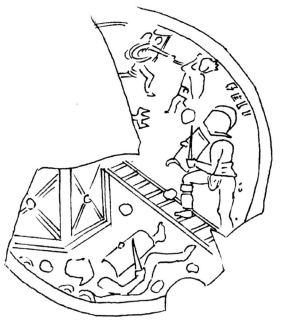

gladiators. Yet it is known that the *retiarius* held the net in his left hand – the *manica* on the left arm prevented the arm from being injured at the moment of the throw, when the *retiarius'* arm was closest to the enemy.

The *pugio* dagger was the third and the least important weapon of a *retiarius*. He held it in his left hand and used it as a last resort, either having lost both the other weapons or in order to deal his adversary a final blow. At any other time there was to no advantage for a *retiarius* to engage in close combat with the *secutor*.

With his armour weighing up to 7–8kg, including a 2–3kg heavy net, the *retiarius* was the most lightly armed gladiator. A heavily armed *secutor*, also called a *contraretiarius*, was his adversary. In combat, this pair represented an encounter between a fisherman (*retiarius*) and a fish (*secutor*). The practice of pairing up differently armed gladiators became particularly widespread in the Imperial period. At that time only a few types of gladiators had similarly armed adversaries (*equites* and *provocatores*). It is possible that before the *secutor* appeared, the *retiarius* was engaged with the *myrmillo*. Very rarely, he might also fight an *arbelas*, a clash that was particularly characteristic of the eastern part of the empire.

The *retiarius* was considered the least prestigious type of gladiator, probably because he lacked heavy ('classical' in Roman interpretation) armament and so had to move incessantly. His combat tactics resembled those of lightly armed

Left:
A tracing from a fragment of a relief from Kos island, at the turn of the 2nd/3rd centuries AD. A *retiarius* and a *secutor* are fighting for the platform. The *retiarius* is holding an indistinct object, perhaps a stick or a throwing spear. (Vladimir Golubev)

Above.
Combat of *pontarii*. Only a point of the trident survives from the figure of a *retiarius*. One of the *secutores* has been knocked down with a hail of stones, the other is still holding up on the steps. Supposedly a combat of *paegniarii* can be seen in the background. A drawing from two fragments of a clay jug, dated 3rd century AD. (Vladimir Golubev)

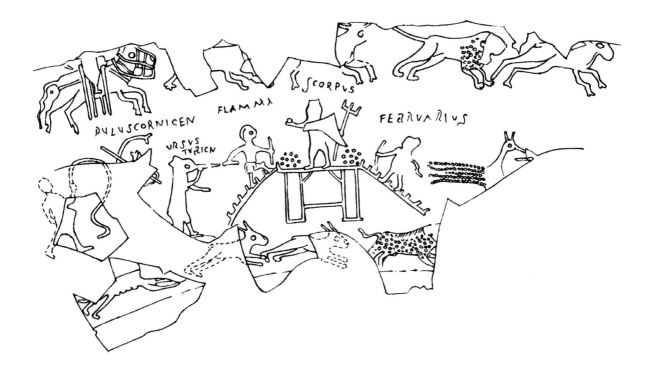

DVLVSCORNICEN

VRSVS TVRICN

FLAMMA

SCORPVS

FEARVARIVS

Attack on the platform (*oppugnatio*) led by two *secutores*. There are two hillocks of stones by the *retiarius*, who is on the defensive. He has already taken a stone into his right hand and is about to launch it. A clay vessel from Langenhain, Wetteraukreis, dated early 2nd century AD. (Vladimir Golubev)

velites (skirmishers) who did not conform to the tactical rules of prestigious Roman legionaries.

A *retiarius* could sometimes oppose two *secutores* at once – he placed himself on a specially raised *pons* platform to make up for being outnumbered. *The pons* was a wooden platform raised to about a man's height above ground. Two narrow inclined boards with steps led up to the platform on two sides. In addition, the *retiarius* was also armed with a store of apple-size round stones. The stones were stored in small pyramids on the platform. As the *secutores* approached the platform and climbed on it, the *retiarius* threw the stones at them. Evidently there was a rule forbidding *secutores* from throwing the stones back at the *retiarius*; without some advantages, the *retiarus* – exposed on the platform and unprotected by a shield or a helmet – would be easy game for the enemy.

Gladiators engaged on the *pons* were also called *pontarii*. No other types of gladiators except a *retiarius* and two *secutores* are known to have fought on the platform. (See reconstruction on page 134.) It seems the platform was sometimes placed in the water-filled arena – the word *pons* (lit. 'bridge') indicates such. It is possible that performances staged on a *pons* surrounded by water led to the representation of a *retiarius* as a fisherman and a *secutor* as a fish.

SECUTOR

The *secutor* (lit. 'persecutor'), also known as *contraretiarius*, was created specially for combat with a *retiarius*. The *secutor* had its origins in the *myrmillo* gladiator, only differing from the latter by the shape of his helmet. His equipment consisted of a helmet, a large rectangular *scutum*, a greave on his left leg, a *manica* on his right arm, and a *gladius* sword.

The *secutor*'s helmet had a streamlined shape, smooth surface, small eyeholes and a fin-like crest. All these features had a double purpose – first protection, to prevent the *secutor*'s head being caught in the *retiarius*' net and to counter the threat from the *retiarius*' trident, and second to call forth an association with a head of a fish. The eyeholes in the *secutor*'s helmet were made very small, no more than 3cm, because a trident could easily pierce through the visor grating in the helmets of all other types of gladiators. For the same reason, there was neither relief decor nor engraving on the *secutor*'s helmet – they could catch on a point of the trident and hence lead to defeat. Helmet brims, which could catch on the net, were also absent.

In action the *secutor* would always try to engage in close combat. He therefore lunged at the *retiarius*, using his large shield for defence. The *retiarius*, by contrast, aimed to keep at a distance and avoid close combat – his main weapons, the net and the trident, were only effective at mid-distance ranges. So the *retiarius* would retreat or whirl round the *secutor*, waiting for the right moment to throw his net over the adversary or use his trident. On account of his much heavier armament, the *secutor* was considerably less mobile. Moreover, his tight, close-fitting helmet with tiny openings for the eyes limited his vision and hearing and, which is even more important, restricted access to fresh air; the *secutor* became tired much sooner than his opponent and had to use his strength sparingly.

A *secutor* was first mentioned late in the 30s of the 1st century AD by Suetonius, who wrote: 'Five *retiarii*, in tunics, fighting in a company, yielded without a struggle to the same number of opponents; and being ordered to be slain, one of them taking up his trident again, killed all the conquerors.' Why the *retiarii* 'yielded without a struggle' remains a mystery. Could it be because Caligula was favourably disposed towards the *secutores* and wished to see them victorious? This is quite possible, considering that in the edict that followed he declared that 'this he lamented as a most cruel butchery, and cursed all those who had borne the sight of it.'[131] Whatever the reason, this occasion shows what a dangerous opponent a *retiarius* could be. *Secutores* were a favourite with Commodus, who would himself often take to the arena as a *secutor*.

Right:
Combat between a *secutor* and a *retiarius* during the 2nd–3rd centuries AD. (Author's reconstruction, artist Vladimir Golubev)

Below:
Decorative bronze figurine shaped as a secutor's helmet, date unknown. (British Museum, London. Author's collection)

THRAEX

The *thraex* (or *thrax*) as a type of gladiator probably appeared in the arena in the first half of the 1st century BC, when a great many Thracians were taken prisoner in the Mithridates' Wars. However the equipment of the *thraex* had little in common with that of the Thracian soldier.

A *thraex* can be easily confused with a *hoplomachus*, as he had similar equipment: a *manica* on his right arm, quilted leg-wrappings, two high greaves and a brimmed helmet with a similar crest. Moreover, the common *thraex*'s adversary was also a *myrmillo*. They were, however, easily distinguished by their shields and their offensive weapons. While the *hoplomachus* used a round shield and attacked with a spear or a straight dagger, the *thraex* protected himself with a small rectangular, almost square *parmula* shield and for attacking wielded a short curved *sica* dagger.

The *thraex*'s helmet was crowned with a peculiar crest in the shape of a griffin's head. The griffin was deemed an incarnation of the goddess of retribution, Nemesis; tiny temples consecrated to the goddess were to be found in many amphitheatres. The crest was adorned with a plume of feathers (*crista*), and a couple of feathers were sometimes added on either side of the helmet. A wide plume of horsehair, however, is never seen on the helmet.

Left:
A *thraex* fighting with a *myrmillo*. *c.* mid-1st century AD. (Author's reconstruction, artist Vladimir Golubev)

Below:
Mosaic from Museo Archeologico, Verona, *c.* AD 200. A *thraex* has mortally wounded a *myrmillo*, whose body is being taken away in a cart that can be seen in the bottom right-hand corner. (akg-images / Cameraphoto)

Measuring roughly 55×60cm, the *parmula* was almost square and with a deeply convex profile. Armed like the *hoplomachus*, with only a small shield, the *thraex* relied on the greaves and the quilted leg-wrappings to protect his legs, which provided covering from the *subligaculum* down to the foot. The *sica*'s blade was normally evenly curved along its length, but after about the mid-1st century AD we also see examples that are more sharply curved around the middle of the blade. With the total weight of his armour reaching 17–18kg the *thraex* fell into the category of heavily armed gladiator. A *myrmillo* was his regular adversary, but there are occasional representations of a *thraex*–*hoplomachus* pair.

Above: Bronze figurine of a *thraex* gladiator. A 'broken' dagger (*sica*) is clearly visible, as are helmet, leg guards and curved shield. (akg-images)

Below: Bronze figurine of a *thraex*. The shield has been broken off; it was larger and of rectangular shape originally. (British Museum, London. Author's collection)

EQUES

Judging by his name (*eques* – rider, pl. *equites*), the *eques* was a mounted gladiator. Yet in the extant images *equites* are usually shown fighting on foot – the *eques* entered combat on horseback, attacking with a spear, and then continued to fight dismounted using a sword. This format is confirmed by several images of the Imperial period, which show mounted *equites* armed with spears. Most artists, however, preferred to depict the final dismounted phase of the combat.

The *eques* wore a broad-brimmed helmet with a visor and often two feathers on either side of the helmet, but without a crest or a central plume. His round, medium-sized *parma equestris* shield was typical for a cavalryman of the Republican period – 60cm in diameter, the shield was made of thick compressed leather. The *eques* protected his right arm with a conventional *manica* and never used greaves, although he wore gaiters and sometimes leg-wrappings. The *hasta* spear was 2–2.5m long and terminated in a leaf-shaped head, and he also fought with the medium-length *gladius* straight sword. As his armour weighed no more than 10–12kg, the *eques* can be classed as a lightly armed gladiator.

Early reliefs show these 'riders' wearing scale armour, while in later images of the Imperial period they wear only voluminous sleeveless tunics. To enable the spectators to tell one adversary from another, the *equites* wore individual multi-coloured tunics or used differently coloured shields. The tunic was secured by a belt on the waist and reached a little higher than the knee.

The *eques* only engaged in combat with his own kind; he never crossed his weapon with any other type of gladiator. A pair of *equites* mounted on white horses opened the programme of gladiatorial games, probably attacking each other from the opposite sides of the arena.

OTHER TYPES

Discussed below are several groups of gladiator about which information is extremely scarce – sometimes there is written evidence but no visual representation, or, the other way around.

ANDABATA

Very little is known about the equipment of this type of gladiator. What we do know for certain is that an *andabata* fought blind – he wore a close helmet that had no apertures for the eyes. He is believed to have worn mail armour on occasions, lest combat should end too soon, and his adversary was another *andabata*.[132] When in combat, an *andabata* had to rely on chance, his ears and the calls of the spectators to secure victory. It is quite probable that the term *andabata* implies not a special type of gladiator, but any type of gladiator wearing a blind helmet and fighting with his characteristic weapon. The *andabata* was no longer found in the Imperial period.

CRUPELLARIUS

This type of gladiator is described only by Tacitus. He says that *crupellarii* were 'clad after the national fashion in a complete covering of steel' and 'though they were ill-adapted for inflicting wounds, they were impenetrable to them.'[133] During the Gallic insurrection of AD 21, *crupellarii* of the Aedui – a tribe of Gallia Lugdunensis, who inhabited the country between the Arar (Saone) and Liger (Loire), in modern France – gave the Romans fierce resistance:

> The men in armour were somewhat of an obstacle, as the iron plates did not yield to javelins or swords; but our men [legionaries], snatching up hatchets and pickaxes, hacked at their bodies and their armour as if they were battering a wall. Some beat down the unwieldy mass with pikes and forked poles, and they were left lying on the ground, without an effort to rise, like dead men.[134]

We can only guess what kind of armour yielded to neither spear nor sword and prevented a warrior from getting on his feet. Even solid European armour of the 15th–16th centuries did not impair movement to such as extreme.

Junkelmann believes that the bronze statuette from Vertigny (Aisne) represents a *crupellarius*.[135] Unfortunately, only a helmet can be clearly seen. This strange headgear, resembling a medieval pot-shaped helmet (Great Helm), seems to have been supplied with numerous apertures for ventilation and a projection in the shape of a nose, probably to facilitate access to fresh air. A strip in the upper part of the helmet could be a vision slit. If, however, it was not a slit, but the joint of two parts of the structure, then it is a representation of an *andabata*. A precise reconstruction of body or leg protection is hardly possible; we can only suggest that it was a sort of laminar structure.

GALLUS

Mentioned in written sources with reasonable frequency, the *gallus* is still one the most enigmatic types of gladiator. It is impossible to identify him definitively with any surviving image, and neither is the exact period of his existence clear.

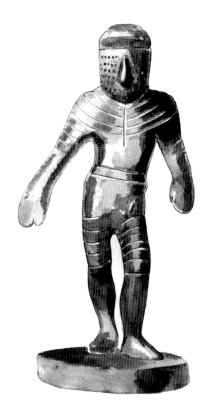

These gladiators seem to have appeared in the early Republican period and disappeared around the mid-1st century BC. Their armour is another puzzle. We can assume that this gladiator resembled the Celts (Gauls) from whom the name of this type of gladiators originated. Therefore, they probably had a large *scutum*, a sword and possibly a helmet and a greave, making the *gallus'* equipment very much like that of the *myrmillo*. The latter appeared in the mid-1st century BC, so it is assumed that a *myrmillo* is simply a renamed *gallus*.[136]

LAQUERARIUS

Most researchers tend to consider the *laquerarius* as a variety of *retiarius*, with the difference that the former used a lasso instead of a net. His weapons were probably a short spear and a dagger.

PAEGNIARIUS

To all appearances, gladiators of this type were not destined for serious combat with the use of sharp weapons. Their task was to entertain the public by parodying combats, putting on their displays between the serious bouts, especially during the midday interval. We have no single

Above: A bronze figurine from Vertigny supposedly representing a *crupellarius*. 1st century AD. (Vladimir Golubev)

Right: A combat of *eques*, 1st–4th centuries AD. (Author's reconstruction, artist Vladimir Golubev)

precise description of *paegniarius'* armour. A suggestion, based on questionable images, is that he had no protection apart from thick quilted wrappings on his legs, left arm and presumably head. His weapons were a stick (sometimes bent at the end) and a whip. *Paegniarii* performed to the accompaniment of cymbals, trumpets and water organs (*hydraulus*). *Paegniarii* were particularly popular during the games staged in the Colosseum by Commodes, and Caligula sometimes had respectable men or maimed persons brought to the arena instead of professional *paegniarii*.[137]

Paegniarii in a mosaic from the Roman villa at Nennig, Saarland, thought to have been produced during the first half of the 3rd century AD. (akg-images)

SAGITTARIUS

As the name suggests (*sagittarius* – archer, shooter), the *sagittarius* was an archer. Iconographic artefacts usually show him holding an intricate composite bow, wearing a conical helmet and scale armour. Written evidence about the *sagittarii* is extremely scrappy and insufficient to create a clear picture of their equipment. Special security measures seem to have been taken during their performances in amphitheatres lest the spectators should find themselves within the range of their bows, which could fire up to 150–200m.

SAMNIS

All the available information about the *samnis* is within the Republican period (the first reference to these gladiators dates from 308 BC), and it appears that the *samnis* was the most popular type of gladiator at that time. The *samnis* came from the warriors of the Samnite tribe defeated by the Romans in the 3rd century BC. Taking a lot of Samnite armour as a trophy, the Romans decorated their forum with it and 'the Campanians … made the gladiators who performed at their banquets wear it, and then they called them "Samnites."'[138]

Samnite armour is minutely described by Livy:

Relief with *sagittarii*. (German Archaeological Institute, Rome)

> There were two divisions; one had their shields plated with gold, the other with silver. The shield was made straight and broad at the top to cover the chest and shoulders, then became narrower towards the bottom to allow it being more easily moved about. To protect the front of the body they wore armour; the left leg was covered with a greave, and their helmets were plumed to give them the appearance of being taller than they really were. The tunics of the men with gold plated shields were in variegated colours, those with the silver shields had tunics of white linen.[139]

Livy's evidence here should be taken with a pinch of salt, however. Modern scholars are inclined to be doubtful about his description of the shield – the few examples discovered point to the Samnites' protecting themselves with a round or large oval shield that possibly had the upper edge cut off. There is a suggestion that Livy's description refers only to *samnis* gladiators, not to Samnite warriors.[140]

Fragmentary evidence and numerous questionable iconographic artefacts reveal that the *samnis*' equipment comprised a helmet with a ridge or feathers, a large oval or rectangular shield, a greave on his left leg, a spear and a sword. They also possibly wore distinctive three-disc armour (composed of three large metal discs).

ESSEDARIUS

The *essedarius* is the most disputed type of gladiator. Although the name *essedarius* (charioteer) comes from *essedum* – a light two-wheel Celtic chariot – there is not a single known image of a gladiator in a chariot that can be matched with this type. The *essedarius* is, however, often recounted in literature and epigraphy, and so he was a familiar figure from at least the mid-1st century BC. The only known image of a gladiator in a chariot represents a warrior armed with a round shield and a spear fighting with a lion.[141] Thus he is a *venator*, not an *essedarius*, which usually fought against another *essedarius*.

As soon as the *essedarius* became a frequent figure in epigraphy, his visual representation must have also become common. Working with this principle,

This reconstruction of an engraving on a tomb stone shows two gladiators in combat, both armed with large shields and javelins, wearing armour and a greave on the left leg, however they have no helmets. Assistants stand behind each gladiator holding three spare javelins each. It is one of those cases where the type of gladiator cannot be determined unequivocally. Some researchers believe them to be *samnites*, (Junkelmann, *Das Spiel mit dem Tod,* p.105) while others see *galli*-gladiators in them (Coarelli, 'L'armamento e le classi dei gladiatori', p.161). Our knowledge of gladiator's armament in the Republican period is insufficient for determining any distinguishing features for these two gladiators. It was believed to have been engraved in the mid-1st century BC. (Vladimir Golubev)

A tracing made in the 19th century from a destroyed relief in Pompeii showing gladiatorial combats. In the upper row there are two *equites*, a *myrmillo–thraex* pair, a *hoplomachus–myrmillo* pair, two *essedarii*, two *retiarii* and a *myrmillo–thraex* pair. The lower row comprises a *myrmillo–thraex* pair and a *thraex–myrmillo* pair as well as some enlarged details of armament. AD 50s. (Nach Mazois 1824)

Junkelmann suggests that any gladiator whose equipment conforms to that of no other type should be assumed to be an *essedarii*.[142] Some images supposedly of *essedarii* are to be found in several reliefs, and they represent combat between two gladiators armed with oval shields and swords, wearing close-fitting helmets with feathers. One relief is particularly interesting. It pictures a group of four men – two are presumably *essedarii* (they cannot be *secutores* judging by their equipment) and two *retiarii*; one of the *essedarii* is finishing off another *essedarius*, with one of the *retiarii* giving him a hand. As *retiarii* never fought against one other, it is likely that the four of them are fighting together in pairs (each pair consisting of a *retiarius* and an *essedarius*). The *essedarius* defeated by a *retiarius* receives a final blow from the opposing *essedarius*, while the defeated *retiarius* takes flight (his figure is reduced in size probably as a perspective technique).

It is, however, inexplicable why *essedarii* should have been made adversaries of *retiarii*. Lacking any greaves and protecting themselves with smaller shields compared with a *scutum*, they would have become easy prey for *retiarii* tridents. This situation can only be explained if the reproduction dates from a time when the *secutor* had not yet become the *retiarius'* classic opponent, and game organizers were experimenting in pairing the *retiarius* off against other types of gladiator. (Similarly, a *myrmillo – retiarius* pair can be seen in earlier images.)

Judging by these images, the *essedarius'* equipment was as follows: a sword, a curved oval shield, a brimless helmet sometimes decorated with two feathers, a *manica* on his right arm and short gaiters on the legs (but no greaves). The total weight of his armour must have reached 10–12kg, so he was a lightly armed gladiator. Junkelmann believes that the *essedarii* sometimes attacked with spears, too,

Two *essedarii* in combat. The one on the right has already raised his finger to show that he is ready to submit. 2nd–3rd centuries AD. (Centre Céramique Maastricht)

and even opened combat by throwing javelins at each other, but as yet we have no primary source confirmation of this idea.[143]

The *essedarius'* method of fighting is also something of a mystery. To all appearances, and despite his name, he fought on foot, not from a chariot. It may be that chariots, which cost a lot of money, fell into disuse while the term survived. Or perhaps the *essedarius* made a pompous entrance onto the arena driving a chariot and then dismounted for combat, in the manner of Homer's heroes. The *essedarius* and his equipment remain an enigma in many respects and require further research.

VELES

Almost nothing is known about the *veles'* equipment. Not a single image has been preserved and only a few inscriptions containing the abbreviation *vel* can be associated with this type of gladiator. We can assume that the *veles* was armed with javelins, a sword and a shield and his fighting methods were similar to those of light infantrymen of the Republic. This assumption is confirmed by the single surviving description of *velites* given by Isidore of Seville, although he lived at the

Fresco from Ashik's crypt, Panticapaeum, 1st century AD. The equipment of these gladiators is strikingly different from that in the west of the Empire at that time. The gladiator on the left is being prepared for combat.

turn of the 6th–7th centuries, that is six centuries after *velites* had disappeared from the arena as well as from the Roman Army.[144]

* * *

Our knowledge of gladiatorial equipment in the Imperial age is sufficient to identify a gladiator's type on about 99 occasions out of a hundred (only considering fully preserved images, that is). There is evidence of a very high degree of standardization in such equipment, with only a few insignificant exceptions. Such is only true for the Mediterranean, however. The lands and peoples at the edges of the Roman Empire had their own particular types of gladiator, of which our knowledge is as yet very limited. Frescos from the so-called Ashik's crypt in Panticapaeum (a region to the north of the Black Sea) are the most striking examples.[145] For example, the gladiators depicted above correspond to no known Western type. The three pairs of gladiators shown in the frescos are armed with short swords, hold small, nearly square, shields with rhomb-shaped *umbos* and wear high conical helmets without visors (some helmets have a small crest). The figures wear nothing but loincloths. None is protected with an arm-guard or a greave, even one made of cloth. One gladiator is holding a trident, but unlike a *retiarius* he has neither a *manica* nor a *galerus*; he is wearing a helmet, though. No gladiators with similar equipment have been found in the west of the empire.

CHAPTER III
THE GLADIATOR'S EQUIPMENT

The distinctive forms of armament and armour worn by each type of gladiator were explained in the previous chapter. In this chapter we will explore in greater depth the structure and evolution of this equipment. First, however, we need to consider what sources or findings are reliable.

Archaeological finds are of paramount importance for understanding the gladiator's armament. Literary descriptions and iconographic artefacts are less valuable, as the former are often extremely scrappy while the latter often show distorted proportions and only give a general impression of the construction of arms and armour. More than 75 per cent of the gladiatorial equipment discovered by post-Roman historians was found in the same place – the gladiatorial barracks (school) in Pompeii. These discoveries were made in 1766–67, and unfortunately archaeological methods were extremely primitive at that time and many objects were not properly described. Some of the findings have also since been lost. Most of the extant remains are in the Archaeological Museum in Naples, although some items were presented to Napoleon in 1802 and are now in the Louvre in Paris. Between them these two museums preserve 15 helmets, five pairs of long greaves, six single short greaves, three shoulder-guards (*galerus*), a small round shield, several daggers and spearheads as well as some fragments of armament.

Most items of this gladiatorial armour (for example, 11 out of the 15 helmets) are opulently adorned with reliefs, so even today many researchers consider them purely ceremonial armour only worn for the ceremony (*pompa*) at the opening of gladiatorial games. Some historians have argued that when gladiators were engaged in combat they wore ordinary unadorned armour, on the basis of the following arguments. First, ceremonial armour is too expensive to expose to the peril of being damaged. Second, most surviving objects of adorned armour (helmets, greaves) have no notches or marks or other damage caused by weapons. Third, richly decorated helmets are too heavy to wear in combat. And fourth, a surface covered with relief work is believed to be too fragile to withstand real blows.

Yet all these arguments are easily unsettled. Gladiatorial games were spectacles aimed at attracting great masses of people, and so gladiators had to look handsome and imposing. Metal playing in the sun, plumes of multi-coloured feathers and armour decorated with reliefs — that was what the public craved. There is another point: gladiators were not numerous (at least compared to the army in the field), and therefore the outlay for even expensive armour could be afforded. No doubt, the luxurious pieces of armour were only supplied for combat and given out right before the performance; they also passed from deceased gladiators to their living comrades, so the *lanista* could make do with only several sets of armour for each type of gladiator. Neither were helmets nor greaves damaged as often as we might assume. A heavy slashing weapon was not used in the arena, and it was impossible to cut through a helmet or greave with a light, short sword. Gladiators directed only light, distracting blows at helmets

Gladiatorial arms and armour pictured on lamps, *c.* 1st century AD. (Römisch-Germanisches Museum, Köln. Author's collection)

or the protected legs of an opponent, not heavy mortal attacks. Distraction blows were most efficient against the visor grating, and therefore that part of the helmet was damaged more often than any other. The visor, however, was the easiest piece to repair at an armourer's shop. Hence it is not surprising that all the discovered helmets and greaves, except one, carry no notches received in fighting. At the same time, a bronze patch can be seen on a helmet that belonged to a *provocator*. Furthermore, only a few *military* helmets of this time, which survive in considerably greater numbers, display damage undoubtedly inflicted by weapons.

The weight of the gladiators' helmets found in Pompeii varies from 3 to 5kg (7–11lb) with an average of 3.8kg.[146] Indeed, they are approximately twice as heavy as the helmet of an ordinary 1st century AD infantryman. It should be remembered, however, that gladiators and legionaries wore their helmets in very different conditions. A legionary protected his head with a helmet while fighting a battle that could last for hours. Moreover, he had to sometimes wear it on a long march (if the enemy was expected to attack at any moment). Therefore the very shape of a legionary's helmet was quite different – close-fitting helmets or restrictive visors were not used, as it is essential for a soldier to have the best possible field of view and to breathe easily. Although as well trained as legionaries, gladiators were not engaged in the arena longer than 10–15 minutes. They entered combat having been properly rested, put on a helmet immediately before going out into the arena and took it off as soon as they finished the fight. Furthermore, the total weight of a

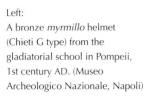

Left:
A bronze *myrmillo* helmet (Chieti G type) from the gladiatorial school in Pompeii, 1st century AD. (Museo Archeologico Nazionale, Napoli)

Right:
A bronze *thraex* helmet (Chieti G type) from the gladiatorial school in Pompeii. 1st century AD. (Museo Archeologico Nazionale, Napoli)

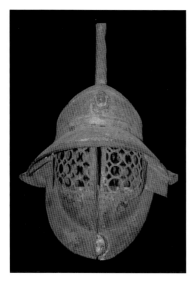
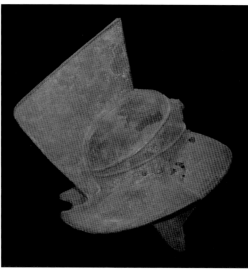

A *myrmillo* helmet (Pompeii G type) adorned with Hercules' image. 1st century AD. (British Museum, London. Author's collection)

legionary's equipment (even excluding the things he needed when on march) reached about 25kg, while a heavily armed gladiator carried no more than 20kg of armament, despite his helmet being twice as heavy.[147]

Another argument made by advocates of purely ceremonial armour is that engraving or embossing decreases the sturdiness of the metal. True, a weapon slides easier along a smooth surface, but a relief surface is considerably harder to cut through (it is not for nothing that many kinds of weapons were specially supplied with stiffening ribs and grooves to add to the hardness of the structure). The bowls of gladiatorial helmets from Pompeii were made from sheet bronze (only one of them was made from iron) as thick as 1–3mm, and 1.5mm thick on average.[148] The visor grating is as a rule 1.8mm thick. All the edges of a helmet are trimmed with metal strips, which makes the metal in these places three or four times thicker. For comparison, the metal in the bowl of a soldier's helmet of the same period (1st century AD) is 1mm thick on average. It can hardly be suggested that Romans equipped their troops with flimsy helmets worthless in real battle. Meanwhile, purely ceremonial, richly adorned helmets were also made of thinner metal, which was much easier to handle.

The most important argument in favour of luxuriously decorated helmets as combat equipment comes from some iconographic artefacts that show gladiators fighting while wearing armour adorned with reliefs. In the reliefs on tombstones from Pompeii and Villa Torlonia, we see decorated helmets, and in the former there is also a *provocator's cardiophylax* plate adorned with the image of the Gorgon's head.

GALEA (HELMET)

A gladiator's helmet of the Late Republic (1st century BC) was, as a rule, a combination of Boeotian and Attic helmet styles. It borrowed its broad, bent-down brim from the former and from the latter took its characteristically shaped forehead plate and wide cheek-guards fastened on hinges. Several reliefs survive that show gladiators and Roman soldiers wearing such helmets. The best one most likely comes from southern Italy, although we cannot say with confidence whether it belonged to a gladiator or soldier, because prior to Emperor Augustus' rule military equipment bore no clear distinction from that of gladiators.

The subsequent evolution of the gladiator's helmet can be traced in the helmets found in Pompeii. They all date from the 1st century AD (Pompeii was buried under ashes following the eruption of Vesuvius in 79) and display a construction that differs notably from that of military helmets. Most of them are comparatively broad brimmed, and based on the shape of the brim can be divided into two types. The first, earlier type (type Chieti G according to Junkelmann) has a horizontal brim all around the perimeter of the helmet. The second one (Pompeii G type) has horizontal brims only on the sides and at the back; at the front the brim is raised sharply over the forehead, forming a characteristic curving peak. This model is a transitional stage towards a later type not represented amongst the finds in Pompeii. This later type (Berlin G) is characterized by a very low (neck level) horizontal brim at the back, plus brims on each side of the helmet and a nearly vertical brim at the front, clearly framing the visor grating. Helmets of the Berlin G type seem to have appeared in the mid-2nd century and remained in vogue up to the last days of the gladiators. Judging by iconographic artefacts, over time these helmets practically never changed in the western empire, while the Hellenistic East saw some modifications (for instance, the narrowing of the brims at the front).

As a matter of fact, the appearance of new types of helmets was by no means closely followed by the disappearance of old ones. It was not by chance that two different types of helmets were found in Pompeii.

A bronze *thraex* helmet (Pompeii G type) from the gladiatorial school in Pompeii. It is recognisable for a characteristic crest in the shape of a griffin's head, thought to be dated 1st century AD. (Museo Archeologico Nazionale, Napoli)

Nor was the Chieti G type ever given up by *equites*, who only stopped wearing it with the end of gladiatorial games. For one century after another (including the 4th century), this helmet remained the *eques'* signature.

In the Imperial period, a gladiator's helmet, whatever the type, was invariably provided with a visor, probably explained by a wish to turn a gladiator into an anonymous combatant whose performance spectators could watch without experiencing excessive sympathy or compassion. The *retiarius*, who wore no helmet at all, was the only exception. A visor consisted of two hinged metal halves and seems to have developed from the cheek-guards of the earlier helmets. Both halves joined at the front, forming a vertical rib. Unlike the visor of late-medieval helmets, a gladiator's visor could not be raised or lowered – it opened out horizontally to the sides. A metal strip forming a noticeable vertical rib protected the place where the two halves of the visor joined together. They were fastened with metal latches on the upper part, which covered the forehead, and sometimes at the bottom, too. But more often the lower part of a visor seems to have been kept in place with the help of leather strap secured though special eyes. The lower parts of both halves were bent outward to protect the throat.

The hinges that held the visor in its place were evidently the visor's Achilles' heel. Any blow struck on the hinges could lead to the loss of the visor. Therefore, special rectangular plates were put on top of the hinges – they can be seen in the area of the temples on most helmets of this type. Not only did they protect the hinges, but they supposedly strengthened the whole structure of the visor.

Early gladiatorial helmets, including the ones discovered in Pompeii, were only supplied with apertures for the eyes. The apertures were round in shape, about 8cm (3in.) in diameter. On the outside, the apertures were often screened with removable round or semi-circular grating-plates.

Beginning from about the end of the 1st century, almost every helmet acquired a visor in the form of a metal grate – only the lower parts of the visor, protecting the neck, remained solid metal. The visor grating also consisted of two halves that joined at the front, forming a vertical rib. The inner and lower edges of the grating were straight, the outer following the contours of the brim of the helmet. To fasten the grating to the helmet each half had two projections, one at the top, the other at the bottom. The projections corresponded to slots in the helmet: at the top there were apertures in the peak, where pintles stabilized the two halves of the grating, and at the bottom the projections were fitted into horizontal slots, in which they could move more or less easily.

Above:
A lamp shaped as a *thraex's* helmet (Berlin G type) with a characteristic crest in the form of a griffin's head. AD 200. (British Museum, London. Author's collection)

Below:
Bronze figurine of a *myrmillo*, 2nd century AD. The sword and shield are gone but the helmet (Berlin G type) is clear. (British Museum, London. Author's collection)

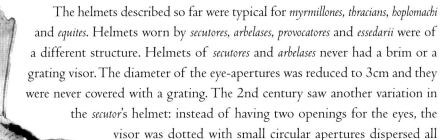

The helmets described so far were typical for *myrmillones*, *thracians*, *hoplomachi* and *equites*. Helmets worn by *secutores*, *arbelases*, *provocatores* and *essedarii* were of a different structure. Helmets of *secutores* and *arbelases* never had a brim or a grating visor. The diameter of the eye-apertures was reduced to 3cm and they were never covered with a grating. The 2nd century saw another variation in the *secutor*'s helmet: instead of having two openings for the eyes, the visor was dotted with small circular apertures dispersed all over the surface (see, for instance, the mosaic from Villa Borghese in Chapter I). This structure provided for easier breathing and possibly an expanded field of vision. Nevertheless, this structure only co-existed with the 'classical' model and never ousted it completely.

Another variety of the *secutor*'s helmet featured a crest extending from the back of the head down to the chin. It can be seen, for example, in a relief from Hierapolis, Asia Minor. The researchers who discovered the relief believe that the crest was probably sharpened for cutting through a net thrown over the *secutor*'s head.[149] Real finds offer no basis for such a conclusion, although all of them date from earlier times and come from Italy.

A *myrmillo* helmet (Berlin G type). Second half of the 2nd–3rd century AD. (Vladimir Golubev)

Helmets of this structure are represented on the small figures and a flask preserved in the Romano-Germanic Museum in Cologne. Some of the objects were found in Cologne; where the others come from is unknown. In the Fitzwilliam Museum, Cambridge, there is another small figure, again of uncertain origins, wearing this helmet. On the whole, we can conclude that helmets like this were widespread, although not very popular in Italy.

At the turn of the first millennium, the *provocator*'s helmet derived from the model common in the Roman Army (Weisenau type). It lacked a visor, and the face was only protected by cheek-guards on either side. During the 1st century AD, this helmet acquired a forehead plate with volutes after the fashion of the Attic helmet, as well as a visor in the Chieti G-style helmets, with circular eye-apertures that could be closed with circular gratings. Following Junkelmann's classification, we call these helmets Provocator G.

In Junkelmann's opinion, the first helmets for *essedarii* date from the early 1st century, and strongly resemble the army helmets of the Mannheim and Haguenau type, but by the second quarter of the 1st century they had already changed their

Relief with a combat between a *retiarius* and a *secutor.* Note the *secutor*'s helmet, with a crest running from the back of the head to the chin. Early 3rd century AD. (Archaeological Museum, Hierapolis. Author's collection)

shape and become nearly identical to the *secutor*'s helmet. Unlike the latter, however, the *essedarius*' helmet lacked a crest but was decorated with two feathers on either side of the bowl.

The helmets of a *myrmillo*, *thraex*, *hoplomachus* and *secutor* were provided with crests. The crescent-shaped crest of the *myrmillo*'s helmet rose vertically at the back, then bent at 90 degrees and continued horizontally to the front. The crest is believed to have symbolized the large dorsal fin of a fish. There was a groove for fixing a plume of horsehair in the *crista* (crest). The *thraex*'s helmet had a curved crest with a griffin's head feature at the front end. A plume of feathers (but not horsehair) could crown the helmet. According to iconographic sources, there was a crest on top of the *hoplomachus*' helmet, too, very much resembling the one on the *thraex*'s helmet. Not a single sample of a *hoplomachus*' helmet has been preserved, however, so the precise shape of the crest remains unknown. The helmets of a *secutor* and *arbelas* were adorned with a narrow crest-ridge without any plume; with the exception of these two, gladiators of all the other types had a couple of bushes on the sides of their helmets in which they stuck *pinnae* (feathers).

Gladiators' helmets were made of bronze, as a rule. Their surface could be simply polished up to play in the sun like gold, or it could be silvered or tinned (covered with a layer of tin, imitating silver). Sometimes part of the surface was

These two figurines of secutores wearing helmets with crests to the chin were discovered in Cologne. (Römisch-Germanisches Museum, Köln. Author's collection)

CHARACTERISTICS OF GLADIATORS' HELMETS, 1ST–4TH CENTURIES AD*

Type of Gladiator	Type of Helmet	Crest	Embossing	Plume (*crista*)	Feathers (*pinnae*)
arbelas	Secutor G	rounded (not always)	–	–	–
eques	Chieti G	–	–	–	+
essedarius	Secutor G	–	–	–	+
hoplomachus	Chieti G (common) Pompeii G (rare) Berlin G (rare)	curved	+	of feathers or horsehair	+
myrmillo	Chieti G Pompeii G Berlin G	in the shape of a crescent, then cut off vertically	+	of horsehair	+
provocator	Provocator G	–	+	–	+
secutor	Secutor G	rounded	–	–	–
thraex	Chieti G Pompeii G Berlin G	curved, with a griffin's head	+	of feathers	+

* + indicates present   – indicates absent

silvered or tinned, the rest left bronze – this format made the helmet appear to be a combination of both gold and silver, a combination dear to the hearts of Romans. In addition, the surface of a helmet was often decorated with reliefs or various subjects executed in deep embossing. Here again the *secutor's* and *arbelas'* helmets were the only exceptions: their surface was invariably smooth.

A helmet must have had internal padding or sat on a padded cap, otherwise the helmet would have transmitted the impact of blows through to the skull. No padding has been preserved, which makes it extremely difficult to ascertain its shape and method of fastening. No surviving helmet has apertures for tying or riveting a fabric lining. Some researchers think that the lining comprised four segments of thick quilted felt glued to the inner side of the helmet.[150] It is, however, more probable that a padding was provided by a quilted arming cap with a cut for the face (like medieval examples) and worn under the helmet. Supporting evidence is found in the picture of a combat between *equites* in a mosaic from the National Archaeological Museum in

A bronze *provocator* helmet from the gladiatorial school in Pompeii, *c.* 1st century AD. (Museo Archeologico Nazionale, Napoli)

Madrid. A fallen *eques* is seen at the top of the picture, with his helmet lying nearby, but a multi-coloured cap is still on the gladiator's head. In this case the arming cap reaches to his shoulders, but evidently it could sometimes reach down as far as the chest. In some pictures, for example the mosaic from Kourion, Cyprus, a layer of cloth falls down from under the helmet upon the gladiator's shoulders and chest.

MANICA (ARM-GUARD)

The left arm of a *retiarius*, and the right arm of gladiators of all other types, was protected with a *manica* arm-guard. (Left-handers naturally wore *manica* the other way around.) A gladiator carrying a moderate size shield (a *hoplomachus*, *eques* and perhaps a *thraex*) occasionally put on two arm-guards to protect both arms, as the shield did not provide for sufficient protection. Later, in the 3rd–4th centuries, the reverse could be seen – some gladiators (*arbelas*, *dimachaerus*) fought without any *manica* at all. However, both these extremes occurred only rarely.

The *manica* probably developed from a *caestus* boxing glove. Fairly short at first, *manica* initially protected only the hand and part of the arm from the wrist to the elbow. Later it was extended up to the shoulder (although the semi-*manica* still made an appearance). A *manica* was usually made of quilted multi-layered cloth or leather. It was held on the arm by numerous leather straps. The arm-guard covered the hand and thumb only on the outside and was fastened there with a leather loop across the fingers. An alternative construction of the *manica* is occasionally seen in images – it was sometimes made of broad leather thongs crossing or overlapping each other. A reconstruction of a long *manica* made of durable fabric, and using horsehair as a filling, shows that such an arm-guard weighed only about 1kg and did not restrict arm movements. At the same time, it could cope effectively with slashing blows, even those struck with a sharp sword – only a thrust inflicted at right angles could do serious harm to the arm.[151]

In the 2nd century, the Romans became acquainted with metal arm-guards – scale, laminar and mail. In the centuries that followed, scale *manicae* undoubtedly became a favourite with gladiators, of which there are numerous depictions. Regarding laminar and mail *manicae*, the extent of their use by gladiators is uncertain. In many cases the available images do not conclusively reveal whether an arm-guard was metal laminar or made of quilted fabric. Only in a mosaic from Kourion (Cyprus) is a *thraex* undoubtedly protecting his right arm with a steel laminar arm-guard, easily recognized by its colour. Generally speaking, laminar arm-guards – made of leather or metal rings, or from semi-rings stringed on vertical cords or sewn onto leather straps – appeared in the 5th century BC and spread amongst the Persians, Scythians and Sakas.[152] The Romans became familiar with such pieces of equipment, but they were not widely used. They used laminar arm-guards for the first time during the Second and Third Dacian Wars (AD 100–102 and 105–106 respectively). Trajan is supposed to have equipped a few of his legions with laminar arm-guards as a means of protection against a horrible sickle-like weapon of the Dacians known as a *falx*. Nevertheless, no laminar arm-guard is to be seen on the Trajan column commemorating his heroic deeds; it is seen only on the Adamklissi Metopes (Tropaeum Traiani), which represent legionaries wearing obsolete armour and laminar arm-guards on their right arms.[153] Fragments of an arm-guard were discovered in Newstead; it comprised horizontal steel bands possibly riveted to leather strips. The mobility of an arm coated in such a *manica* probably left much to be desired, until, that is, a detached elbow-protecting plate was devised as an additional structural feature. The 2nd Legion Augusta re-enactment group set out to discover the way the plates in a laminar *manica* overlapped – from top to bottom or from bottom to top. Having reconstructed the two types and tested them in a fight, they came to the conclusion that both variants were used, depending on the enemy's weapon.[154] No indisputable image of a gladiator's mail arm-guard has yet been discovered.

Metal *manicae* never ousted the leather or cloth varieties. Scale and either leather or cloth arm-guards are represented in the mosaic from Villa Borghese, dating from the early 4th century AD. A metal *manica* was fastened with belts running across the breast, back and the left shoulder. A quilted fabric wrapping was undoubtedly worn under this arm-guard. *Paegniarii* and *bestiarii* also protected their left arms with quilted wrappings, but these wrappings differed from *manica* – they were much thicker and seem to have covered the arm and hand together.

OCREA (GREAVES)

Greaves were not common items in the Roman Army in the Late Republican or the Imperial periods. Only centurions wore them more or less regularly. Gladiators' greaves are probably derived from the Greek hoplites' greaves of the Archaic period (8th–5th centuries BC). However, a hoplite's greave often protected his leg at the

Bronze greaves of *myrmillones* or *secutores* from the gladiatorial school in Pompeii, *c.* 1st century AD. (Museo Archeologico Nazionale, Napoli)

back as well as at the front. Perfectly fitted to the leg, it required no strings at all. A gladiator's greave was quite different. It protected the shin only at the front and a little on either side. Each greave had several pairs of rings (two to four); leather straps were threaded through these rings and tied at the back.

Greaves differed in size depending of the type of gladiators. A *thraex* or *hoplomachus* protected his legs with greaves reaching up above the knees, while a *myrmillo* or a *secutor* wore the shortest greaves, only covering the shins. A *provocator's* medium-sized greaves did not reach higher than his knees. The size of the greaves was probably directly related to the size of the shield – gladiators armed with larger shields (a *myrmillo* or a *secutor*) could make do with a short shin defence, while those using small shields (a *thraex* or a *hoplomachus*) needed high greaves. In addition, a distinctive bend of the upper edge of the greaves worn by *myrmillones* and *secutores* may have protected their legs from being hit by the bottom edge of their own shields. At the same time, it remains inexplicable why gladiators fighting with no shield at all (an *arbelas* or a *dimachaerus*) made do with only short greaves. If a *retiarius* could compensate for the lack of greaves by using a long weapon such as trident,

THE CHARACTERISTICS OF GLADIATORIAL GREAVES, 1ST–4TH CENTURIES AD				
Type of Gladiator	Type of Greave	Number of Greaves	Average Height	Average Weight (one item)
arbelas	short	pair	31.5cm*	1kg*
dimachaerus	short	pair	31.5cm	1kg*
hoplomachus	high	pair	55cm	2.2kg
myrmillo	short	one, on the left leg	31.5cm	1kg
provocator	mid-height	one, on the left leg	48cm	1.7kg
secutor	short	one, on the left leg	31.5cm	1kg
thraex	high	pair	55cm	2.2kg
essedarius, eques, retiarius	no greaves	–	–	–
*Indicates that no original samples have been found and the given numbers are estimated.				

which allowed him to hold his adversary at a sufficient distance, there is no explanation why an *arbelas* or *dimachaerus*, equipped with weapons for close combat only, should not have worn high greaves. The gladiators of these two types wore scale armour or a mail shirt reaching only as far down as mid-thigh; their unprotected knees must have made an excellent target. It is equally surprising that *essedarii* and *equites* wore no greaves.

Thracians, *hoplomachi* and *arbelases* wore greaves on both legs, while *myrmillones*, *secutores* and *provocatores* had only one greave on the left leg. A short greave had a characteristic U-shaped cut at the bottom end. There was no such cut in a high greave.

A gladiator's greaves were made from a single piece of bronze. Their surface could be plain or liberally adorned, mostly with embossing, engraving or perforation. A greave reaching above the knee had a projection for the kneecap.

Quilted fabric wrappings known as *fasciae* were worn under the greaves. *Fasciae* reached as high as the knees or, when worn with high greaves, up to the loincloth. They served as a lining for the greaves and gave an additional protection for the leg at the same time. They also prevented a leg from being rubbed sore and made greaves more comfortable to wear. Reconstructed highly quilted *fasciae* weigh up to 3.5kg.[155]

About half the greaves, as well as many gladiators' helmets, carry inscriptions. Some of them (for example, 'N.C.A.', 'NER.', 'NER. AVG.') may have indicated that they had been made at an Imperial gladiatorial school (Nero's school in this case). They indicate that there were armour-producing shops within the big schools.

Bronze greaves of either *thracians* or *hoplomachi* gladiators, from the gladiatorial school in Pompeii, 1st century AD. (Museo Archeologico Nazionale, Napoli)

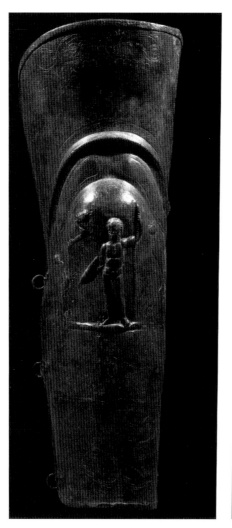 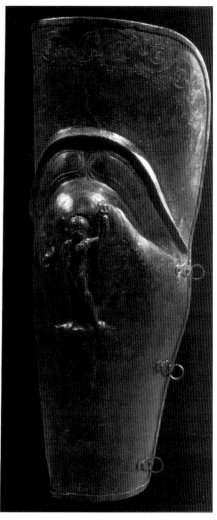

Some of the products from these shops were used to equip the gladiators of the school, while the rest was offered for sale (the above-cited inscriptions were discovered on military equipment in Pompeii). Inscriptions of other sorts could have been made by private producers of weapons or by the *lanistae* of a gladiatorial school. Thus, the inscription 'M.C.P.' (Marcus C.P.) can be seen on ten identical armour pieces that obviously could not belong to one and the same gladiator. On the whole, strange as it may seem, no inscriptions made by the users (gladiators) have been discovered yet. In this, gladiatorial armour differs considerably from military items, which fairly often carried soldiers' signatures, sometimes even the names of several users on one item.[156]

SHIELDS

The shield of the *myrmillo* and *secutor* was a copy of the Roman infantryman's *scutum*, used by legionaries. Therefore, gladiatorial shields changed along with developments in the army shield. During the Republic and Early Empire, the *scutum* had an oval form, but from approximately the mid-1st century AD it becomes rectangular. Generally, it was 100–130cm high and 60–80cm wide. The shield had a semi-cylindrical shape – its sides bent inwards – which provided for better defence than a flat shield. It was made like a plywood sheet, from two or three layers of wood glued perpendicular to each other. On its outside, the shield was covered with leather or felt, and it was edged with bronze or iron strips. A vertical wooden rib (*spina*) ran along the entire shield, providing additional structural strength. In the centre of its outer surface there was a bronze or iron oval boss (*umbo*). Cut out in the shield just behind the boss was a circular opening containing a horizontal hilt. The outer surface of the *scutum* was covered with a decorative or metaphoric ornament.

In many images of legionaries and gladiators, their shields look small in size. The height of the *myrmillo* or *secutor*'s *scutum*, however, can be calculated based on the size of the greaves. In the main stance – left shoulder and left leg brought forward towards the opponent – the shield was to protect the gladiator's body from the greaves to the chin. Moreover, the greave and the shield overlapped by at least 10cm to provide sufficient protection for the left leg against, first, the enemy's weapon and second, from blows struck against the leg by one's own shield. Hence the height of the shield varied depending on the height of its owner, but it was rarely less than 100cm.

A reconstruction of a *scutum*, made by P. Connolly on the basis of a shield found in the Fayum Oasis in Egypt (128×63.5cm in size), weighed a little more than 10kg. The reconstruction of a shield from Doncaster was approximately as heavy.[157] Even if the gladiatorial *scutum* supposedly weighed a little less (say, 6–8kg[158]), still it is obvious that one had to have uncommon bodily strength and training to operate a heavy shield like that, especially holding it by one hilt in the centre. For a legionary acting in close order, handling the *scutum* was easier than for a gladiator, who needed very high mobility and speed in operating his shield, which was particularly difficult considering its weight.

The *provocator*, who had a higher greave, could do with a shorter *scutum*, about 70–80cm high, and slightly pointed at the top and bottom edges. For a long time the oval *scutum* stayed in service with the *essedarii* – it can be seen in images dated as late as the 2nd–3rd centuries. At the beginning of the 1st century, *essedarii*'s shields may have been

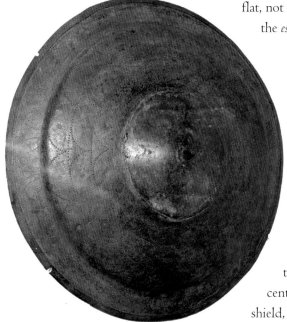

Hoplomachus bronze shield. 1st–2nd centuries AD. (British Museum, London. Author's Collection)

flat, not curved, which is characteristic of Celtic tradition to which the *essedarii* trace their origin.[159]

The small shield of the *hoplomachus*, made of one piece of bronze, was round and markedly curved. This shield, probably like the *thraex*'s shield called *parmula*, was much smaller than its prototype – the hoplite's shield. In some representations *hoplomachus'* shields look unusually bulging. Meanwhile, extant round *parmulae* are rather flat, sometimes with alternating concentric circles of stiffening ribs and grooves. The opulently decorated sample from Pompeii is 37cm in diameter while the degree of its curvature reaches only 5cm in the deepest place. The metal is 1.42mm thick. The entire weight of the shield is 1.6kg. There is a wide bronze stripe in the centre of the shield, on its inner side. Probably to hold the shield, the *hoplomachus* passed his forearm through this central hilt and his hand gripped a leather loop fixed on the rim of the shield. This way the *hoplomachus* could hold his minor weapon – a dagger – in his left hand while operating a spear with his right arm. If the spear was lost, the gladiator put his dagger in his right hand and used the left hand to hold the shield by the central hilt.

The fairly small shield of the *thraex* (the *parmula*) was nearly square in outline and markedly curved in cross section. Like the *scutum*, it was made of a few perpendicularly placed layers of wood and topped with leather. Judging by the proportions shown in images, it was approximately 55×60cm. It is difficult, however, to rely on fine arts in this matter – sizes vary considerably as artists rarely observed proportions. There is an opinion that the size of a *thraex'* or *hoplomachus'* shield can be calculated on the basis of the images on large shields discovered in Dura-Europos. The excavations of this city revealed both oval and rectangular *scutum* shields richly adorned on the outer sides. Most important to us is that in the central part of the shields there is a decorated circle (if the shield is oval) and a decorated rectangle (if the shield is rectangular). I. V. Akilov has suggested that the sizes of these decorated pictures were not accidental, and that they correspond to the real sizes of small gladiatorial shields.[160] Calculations made for the *hoplomachus'* circular shield on the basis of proportional sizes, and comparison of the results with the size of the surviving samples, have confirmed the theory's accuracy. Thus rated, the size of a *thraex*'s shield should be about 40×50cm.

CHARACTERISTICS OF GLADIATORIAL SHIELDS.[161]			
Type of Gladiator	Type of the Shield	Approximate Sizes	Approximate Weight
eques	*parma equestris*	60cm diameter	1.9kg
essedarius	oval *scutum*	100×50cm	6kg
hoplomachus	round *parmula*	35–40cm diameter	1.5–2kg
myrmillo	oval, then rectangular *scutum*	100–110cm high, 60–65cm wide along the chord, about 80cm along the arc of the circumference	6–8kg
provocator	*scutum* with pointed top and bottom edges	70–80cm high, 50cm wide	4–5kg
secutor	rectangular *scutum*	100–110cm high, 60–65cm wide along the chord, about 80cm along the arc of the circumference	6–8kg
thraex	square or rectangular *parmula*	55×60cm (or 40×50cm)	3kg
arbelas, dimachaerus, retiarius	no shield	—	—

The *parmula* usually lacked the classical circular boss (*umbo*), and the vertical *spina* was not very common either. Both the examination of iconographic artefacts, and a tentative reconstruction, have revealed that the hilt was placed vertically in these shields. The reconstructed *parmula* is as heavy as 3kg.[162]

The *equites'* shield (*parma equestris*) had a completely different structure. It was a medium-sized round shield traditionally used by the cavalry of the Republican period. About 60cm in diameter, the shield was made of thick compressed leather. A reconstruction of such a shield, proposed by Junkelmann, was achieved based on similar Turkish shields dating from the 17th–18th centuries. About 4cm thick, strengthened with concentric bulges, the shield could successfully

Bronze spearheads found in the gladiatorial school in Pompeii. The three-edged head (second from left) was probably one of the points of a *retiarius'* trident, *c.* 1st century AD. (Museo Archeologico Nazionale, Napoli)

withstand a blow, was easy to use and highly manoeuvrable. As not one example of an *equites'* shield survives, and iconography fails to offer sufficient information, the structure of the grip is not clear. Junkelmann suggests a structure similar to the Turkish shields: a central grip consisting of crossed straps and additional loops at the sides of the shield.[163] This structure allowed two types of grip: a horseman could let his arm pass first through the central hilt and then through an additional loop at the side of the shield (the same hand would hold the rein); when fighting on foot the gladiator could grip the shield by the central hilt only.

Up to the mid-1st century, *venatores* were also equipped with shields. Various types of shields for *venatores* are in representations: rectangular, round and oval. Some of them were provided with a boss, others were not. These shields were made of wood, bronze or compressed leather, and there might also have been wicker shields. Often the same picture shows *venatores* with different shields, as seen in various photographs in this book. For example, in one image the *venatores* are armed with round, rectangular, and nearly square shields, while in another they have two types of shield – a large oval or rectangular *scutum* and a fairly small, almost round, shield. The variations suggest a lack of standardization in *venatores'* equipment at the time. From the second half of the 1st century, *venatores* were only equipped with a spear, as a rule, but occasionally a *venator* is depicted with a shield.

WEAPONS

In the Early Republican period, a gladiator seems to have used a *hasta* (spear) as his main weapon, but in the Late Republican and Early Imperial periods the spear becomes a rarer weapon in the arena. This evolution is supported by iconographic artefacts; though a considerable number of spearheads were discovered in the gladiatorial school in Pompeii. In the Imperial period, spectators saw a spear only in the hands of a *hoplomachus*, *eques*, *venator* or possibly an *essedarius*. The spear slightly exceeded a man's height and was about 200–230cm long. All the surviving spearheads are made of bronze and have sockets that fit on the shafts; the blade was usually of a broadleaf, lanceolate or, more seldom, a triangular shape. In some representations of a *venatio* – for instance, in the mosaic from Villa Borghese – *venatores'* spears have a crosspiece below the spearhead; the points of the crosspiece were bent down. This crosspiece served as an arresting device to prevent the weapon from piercing too deep into an animal's body. Animals in this mosaic, however, are shown pierced right through, with the spearhead together with the crosspiece coming out of the other side, although this depiction is probably just artistic license.

Beginning in the Late Republican period, a gladiator's predominant weapon is the Spanish *gladius* (*gladius hispaniensis*) – a straight sword with a longitudinal stiffening rib and a clearly marked point. It could be applied for cutting slashes, but it was even better at thrusting. This sword had been adopted as the main weapon of the Roman Army in the late 3rd century BC, and it is to the name of this sword that we owe the term 'gladiator'.

The Spanish *gladius* had a straight, 62–66cm long and 4–5.5cm broad, double-edged blade with a clearly marked point. Towards the late 1st century BC, it became shorter and the form of its blade changed – now the sword was approximately 50cm long with a broad double-edged blade up to 8.7cm wide. The blade was broadest by the handle, then narrowed slightly and then widened again; in the last third of its length it smoothly narrowed down towards the point. The total length of the weapon was about 75cm. The handle was usually made of ivory; the guard and the pommel of wood; there were sometimes all-wooden or all-ivory sword-hilts, too. Known today as the Mainz type *gladius*, this weapon lasted until the mid-1st century AD, when it was ousted by the so-called Pompeii type *gladius*. The new sword had a shorter (about 45cm) and narrower (5–6cm) double-edged blade, with both sides of the blade first running parallel to each other and then turning at 45 degrees towards the point. The weight of the Mainz type *gladius* was about 1.1–1.3kg, and the Pompeii type weighed about 1kg.

A wooden training dagger *sica* (curved dagger used by a *Thracian* gladiator), discovered in the legionary camp of Oberaden, north Germany. Late 1st century BC. (akg-images / Peter Connolly)

In addition, numerous images, especially those made after the mid-1st century, show a gladiator armed with a shorter sword, which judging by its proportions had a blade not exceeding 30cm. Either it is the product of artistic license, or most gladiators were now armed with daggers instead of swords. Three daggers with straight blades, diamond-shaped in cross-section, were found in the gladiatorial school in Pompeii. The blades were 19.5, 20 and 29.7cm long, the corresponding length of the daggers being 30.3, 30.5 and 41cm respectively. Such daggers were mostly used by *retiarii* and *hoplomachi*, but may have been used by gladiators of other type, as well. They were designed almost exclusively for thrusting. There is a possibility that some gladiators also used swords designed only for cutting, with no point at all. Such a weapon can be seen in the hands of an *essedarius* and an *eques* in some representations; it could be another example of artistic license, however.

Thracians were distinguished by the curved *sica* dagger. Until the mid-1st century, all types of *sica* had a blade evenly curved along its length, but in later examples the blade could be sharply 'broken' (at about 45 degrees) in the middle. *The sica* was possibly double-edged and designed mainly for thrusting, although it could slash and even cut in case of a 'broken' blade. A wooden *sica* used in training and discovered in a legionaries' camp in Oberaden is 46.5cm long, with a 'blade' as long as 30.5cm.[164] At the same time, an iron-bladed example of the weapon, also considered a variety of the *thraex'* *sica*, is much longer: it is 60cm long with a blade of up to 45cm.[165]

Around the turn of the 2nd century, a Roman infantryman's *gladius* gradually gave way to the longer *spatha*. In the 3rd century, the *spatha* was in widespread use. Its blade was considerably longer than that of a *gladius*; it was typically as long as 70.5cm, but sometimes reached 85cm. It was owing to the growing popularity of the *spatha* that gladiators sometimes armed themselves with this sword. These gladiators were called *spatharii*. Epigraphic data informs us that there were *myrmillones-spatharii*, *provocatores-spatharii* and even *thracians-spatharii*.[166] The existence of the latter is especially surprising, as a *thraex* is known for his indispensable curved *sica*. Taking this fact into account, some researchers tend to consider the term *spatharius* as indicating the rank of a gladiator rather than characterizing his weapons, and even suggest replacing it with another term (for example, *spectatus*).[167]

As we have seen, the *retiarius* employed a net as one of his weapons. As it was essentially a throwing weapon, it was sometimes called *jaculum* – a 'throwing missile' – and a *retiarius* was called *jaculator*. The rare surviving images of a net allow us to come to some conclusions concerning its structure and size. To all appearances, it was a round net, 3–4m in diameter, with wide cells (10–20cm). Experimental reconstruction of the net reveals that it must have had small lead weights along the perimeter. The weight of such a net was 1.5–3kg.[168]

We have already noted that judging by the images of *retiarii* a net rarely played a conclusive part in the encounter. More often than not, by the final round of the combat a *retiarius* was no longer holding the net. At this stage the *fuscina* trident was deployed as the main weapon. A trident must have been 1.6–1.8m long and it ended with a small three-pointed head that probably had no barbs. A three-pointed head of a trident dating back to the 2nd or 3rd century was found in the port of Ephesus (Asia Minor). Its points are nearly circular in section and as big as 12–15mm in diameter; they are only 50mm apart.[169] It was probably the head of an ordinary fishing trident, not a gladiator's weapon. Gladiators' tridents, however, were hardly different from fishing tridents – the distance between the points was about the same, judging by the extant images.

OUTFIT

Gladiators generally wore nothing except a loincloth and a belt, a tradition that was probably rooted in the nakedness of the heroic Greek athletes. The Roman public undoubtedly enjoyed the sight of a powerful gladiator's torso, the play of muscles and a breast open to blows. The combination of a bare torso, a close helmet and an arm-guard was only typical of gladiators. A Roman soldier displayed a completely opposite tendency – his body was usually clad with some kind of armour, he had no arm-guards, and his military helmet was open and of the lightest variety.

A *subligaculum* loincloth had the shape of an isosceles triangle. It was put on in the following way: first, leaving one end to hang down at the back, the other two ends were wound round the waist and knotted at the front; then the hanging end was passed between the legs and through the knot, allowing the cloth to hang loosely at the front. Modern experiments have shown that a *subligaculum* would have been 1.5m wide at the least.[170]

The belt worn on top of a loincloth was usually fastened at the back. The gladiatorial *balteus* belt can be traced back to an ancient south Italian custom. Already worn among the Samnites, Campanians, Lucanians and Apulians, this belt was an indispensable attribute of any adult male. As wide as 8–12cm, the belt was typically a bronze band on a leather lining. It was fastened with two hooks slotted into the corresponding holes on the opposite side. There were usually three pairs of holes on the belt, so it was no trouble to fit it to any figure. The 2nd–3rd centuries saw a broad, probably leather, sash worn beneath the *balteus*. In the Late Empire, a belt called *cingulum* consisting of ring-clasps was frequently worn instead of a *balteus*.

Gladiators usually fought barefoot. Junkelmann, however, believes that they often wore leather, laced semi-boots that had no sole.[171] Gladiators often tied a leather strap round the leg that was unprotected by a greave, just below the knee. It must have served in a similar way to a wristband worn by athletes today, protecting the muscles from strains and sprains. Small tassels or laces tied to a wristband are visible in some images, each gladiator having a different number of tassels. There is a supposition that the number of tassels equalled the number of victories won by the gladiator.[172]

Although gladiatorial clothing could be limited, the Roman moral code stood against complete nakedness and also against displaying bare female breasts, so women gladiators covered them with a *strophium* band. An *eques* was the only gladiator who always concealed his torso – he is invariably seen wearing a tunic in all images. Tunics could vary in colour and usually had two vertical stripes, *clavi*, of a colour different to that of the tunic. *Equites* seem to have always remained conservative and indifferent to fashion; at least there are no images in which they are depicted wearing the luxuriously embroidered tunics that *venatores* wore in the later times. Judges invariably wore white tunics with *clavi*.

Apart from *equites*, *venatores* and *bestiarii*, gladiators of some other types, particularly *retiarii*, are occasionally depicted wearing something resembling a tunic, typically a kind of semi-tunic usually covering only the left part of the body. *Retiarii* are sometimes described as wearing tunics;[173] perhaps it is to these gladiators that the term *retiarii tunicati* was applied.[174] Some images show a *venator* wearing scale armour (*lorica squamata*); these images are extremely rare, though. A gladiator is often depicted with a breastplate; clearly a result of Etruscan influence, this plate (*cardiophylax* or *pectorale*) was also a characteristic feature of a *provocator*.

CHAPTER IV
METHODS OF COMBAT

Unlike medieval treatises on swordsmanship, no treatise on the martial skills of either gladiators or Roman legionaries survives, and probably none were written. It is only possible, therefore, to reconstruct gladiatorial tactics on the basis of iconographic artefacts and the general characteristics of a certain sort of weapon. This approach will inevitably be full of guesswork and will hardly ever give a complete picture of a gladiatorial fight. We shall, however, try to pick out some specific peculiarities characteristic of at least the main types of gladiator.

On first appearances, a gladiator's defensive armament may appear inadequate, leaving the fighter fairly vulnerable. This is not so, however. As we have seen, most gladiators received protection from helmets, greaves, quilted wrappings, *manicae* and shields. Only the torso of a gladiator usually remained bare. Anyone who has ever attempted swordplay knows how difficult it is to strike a blow on the opponent's chest or belly – such attacks are only easy in the movies. Arms and legs are the most accessible targets; the head is less vulnerable. Human remains found on battlefields confirm this picture: most skeletons have damaged limb bones. It is likely that the first blows in any type of fighting were aimed at the enemy's extremities in an attempt to deprive him of movement or the use of his weapons. Only once those objectives were secured was the opponent killed with a blow to the head or the torso.

Had gladiators fought practically unprotected, combat would have ended too quickly, or would have bored the spectators as the opponents avoided approaching each other. Yet a gladiator's arms, legs and head were well protected, so excluding a quick and easy victory, gladiatorial armament provoked gladiators into an aggressive style of fighting. Romans did not care for a short-lived combat; they wanted to see a showy battle full of powerful strikes.

We have seen how gladiators differed greatly in their types of armament. Romans, especially during the Imperial period, liked to play off different types of gladiators against one another, while at the same time trying to prevent one type dominating another. A *retiarius*, for instance, had three offensive weapons but lacked many elements of defence. The small shield of a *thraex* or a *hoplomachus* was counterbalanced with high greaves protecting his legs. A *myrmillo*, *provocator* and *secutor* protected themselves with a big shield, but had only one short greave on the left leg.

The gladiators' short swords did not allow gladiators to fence in our sense of the word. The parrying of blade by blade was evidently an exceptional manoeuvre. Thrusting attacks considerably outnumbered cutting ones, a fact revealed both by the starting position of the opponents and the sort of wounds that can be seen in iconographic sources. Blows were warded off with a shield rather than the sword, and as in medieval fighting, a shield could be an offensive weapon, too, when a blow was struck with its plane or edge. All gladiators had a repertoire of tricks and dummy blows as well.

It would be incorrect, though, to assume that fencing skills were primitive or underdeveloped. It is only natural that a man equipped with a shield would try to protect himself with the shield, not a sword. When, however, he had no shield, a gladiator had to fence in the manner we know today. Formal fencing skills certainly existed in antiquity, and at least two types of gladiator – the *dimachaerus* and the *arbelas* – must have used blades both offensively and defensively.

A left-handed gladiator held his weapon in his left hand and was called *scaeva* (left-hander); such is often reflected in inscriptions, for example: *mur* (millo) *scaev* (that is a 'left-handed *myrmillo*'). Emperor Commodus is known to have been a left-handed *secutor*.[175] A fight between two left-handed fighters was called *pugna scaevata* (a combat of left-handers). Some gladiators knew how to fight with multiple kinds of weapon. For instance, a gladiator called Hermes could fight with a spear (possibly as a *hoplomachus*) and a trident (a *retiarius*):

Hermes is the pride of his age in martial contests; Hermes is skilled in all kinds of arms; Hermes is a gladiator and a master of gladiators; Hermes is the terror and awe of his whole school; Hermes is he of whom alone Helius is afraid; Hermes is he to whom alone Advolans submits; Hermes is skilled in conquering without a blow; Hermes is his own body of reserve; Hermes makes the fortunes of the letters of seats; Hermes is the object of care and anxiety to the actresses; Hermes walks proudly with the warlike spear; Hermes threatens with Neptune's trident; Hermes is terrible with the helmet shading the face; Hermes is the glory of Mara in every way; Hermes is everything in himself and thrice a man.[176]

In the following quotation, a young woman criticizes her lover in a papyrus, noting him as a gladiator who fought with both a *myrmillo*'s and a *retiarus*' weapons:

> But by the order of an arrogant man you fell down, oh, *myrmillo*,
> With only a sword gripped in your hands.
> As a *retiarius* with a trident you were skilful too.
> You are gone and left me alone, and now my lot is poverty and fear…[177]

The remains of 68 gladiators recently discovered in a cemetery in Ephesus (Asia Minor) allow us to reach some conclusions concerning gladiators' head injuries. Sixty-six of the skeletons belonged to men who died at 20–30 years old, while one belonged to a 45 to 55-year-old man and one to a woman. Twenty-one skeletons (31 per cent) had head injuries. In the case of 11 skeletons (16 per cent), head injuries did not cause death – they healed in the men's lifetime and were very well treated, which is evidence of the high level of medical care given to gladiators. Six out of the 11 skeletons had only one head injury and five had numerous traumas. Of the 16 injuries in total, researchers associate seven (44 per cent) of them with blows struck with blunt objects (presumably resulting from an impact dent on the helmet or a blow dealt with a wooden training weapon), four (25 per cent) with a sharp weapon (presumably a cutting blow with a sword or dagger) and five (31 per cent) with a thrusting weapon that did not penetrate deep into the skull. Out of the latter five, two were supposidly caused by swords or daggers, another two by tridents and one by an unidentified object. Most of the injuries (69 per cent) are on the front part of the head, the rest are to be found on both sides of the skull in more or less equal numbers. There were no traumas to the back of the head.

Ten skeletons (15 per cent) had traces of mortal wounds to the head. Three (30 per cent) were inflicted with blunt objects (such as a shield or a wooden training weapon) and seven (70 per cent) with a sharp object that penetrated through the skull bone. The apertures of the seven penetration traumas are of different shapes: rhombic, triangular, circular and oval. Researchers suppose that one of the wounds was inflicted with a sword or dagger, another with a javelin or a spear, one more with

A duel between a *secutor* and *retiarius* pictured on a flask. The *secutor's* helmet has a crest running to the chin and numerous tiny round apertures. (Römisch-Germanisches Museum, Köln. Author's collection)

a trident (two wounds, to be exact, 5cm apart, which is a common distance between the points of a trident) and the remaining four with hammers. Among the mortal wounds, only 20 per cent were dealt to the front of the head and the remaining 80 per cent to the sides of the head, divided equally between each side. Again, there were no traumas of the back of the head.[178]

The number of mortal wounds on the head may seem surprisingly high considering that gladiators of most types wore helmets. The authors of the research brought forward a hypothesis that most of these traumas can be accounted for by the fact that the gladiators were finished off with a hammer (according to a mention by Tertullianus[179]). Yet this method of dispatch was only applied to condemned criminals, not to professional gladiators. Therefore, if the deaths of those four men were really caused by hammer blows, we would have to admit that criminals sentenced to be killed with a sword were buried in the cemetery at Ephesus – yet it seems improbable that criminals were buried in a graveyard (or, moreover, with a tombstone). On the basis of surviving iconography, a professional gladiator received a final blow to the throat or on the chest, delivered by his opponent using a dagger. So there could be four possible explanations for the mortal head wounds, where a professional gladiator is concerned. First, the wound could be the result of a chance trauma received in the course of training, when helmets were worn only occasionally, mainly in the early stages of instruction. Second, *retiarii*, who never wore helmets, may have been numerous in Ephesus. Third, a gladiator could lose his helmet in combat, which is confirmed by a mosaic from the National Archaeological Museum in Madrid depicting a duel between *equites*. Finally, there is a possibility that gladiators of other types sometimes fought in the arena without helmets. Perhaps a gladiator sometimes went bareheaded in the hope of winning the support of the spectators. At least one such instance is known, though it cannot be ruled out that only a voluntary gladiator could refuse to wear a helmet.[180]

The lack of wounds to the back of the head shows that the gladiator never turned his back to the enemy. In most images a gladiator is shown standing in the

A mosaic showing combat between a *retiarius* and a *secutor* in the presence of an umpire (*summa rudis*), early 3rd century AD. Both gladiators are holding a classical stand: left leg in front, right leg behind, almost straight, torso is vertical and half-turned towards the opponent. (akg-images)

left-hand forward position, the torso straight or slightly bent and turned at 45 degrees towards his adversary. His left leg (more rarely the right leg) is placed forward and bent so that the knee is overhanging the centre of the foot; the right leg, almost straight, is left behind. The length of the stance (the distance between the feet) is about one and a half times the width of his shoulders. This position appears to be the predominant stance for all types of gladiator. It is also known in Japanese martial arts, where positions such as *zenkutsu-dachi* (feet are at the width of the shoulders) or *seigon* (feet aligned) are assumed. Unfortunately, iconography gives us no answer about the width of the stance – whether the feet were in line or set at the width of the shoulders. Any causal connection with Japanese martial arts is obviously out of the question; the similarities occur simply because the stance is so practical and used in many kinds of single combat.

The stance is solid and manoeuvrable and allowed the gladiator to both deliver powerful strikes and ward them off. It was especially convenient for gladiators manipulating a big *scutum*. Holding the shield vertically, covering from the helmet to the greave on the left leg, a gladiator protected practically all his body. The shield was held close to the torso, while the right hand with a sword was at the ready by the right hip. In this position the gladiator would try to approach his adversary and close the distance enough to make a thrust or a cutting blow. Making a lunge, he had to expose his body and was for a moment extremely vulnerable to a counter-attack. Such is why a gladiator is sometimes shown making a thrust over the edge of his own shield; this technique, however, demanded an excellent sense of timing and a short distance of attack. Most frequently a gladiator seems to have attacked by holding his shield slightly aside and turning or making a step forward. An experienced fighter probably knew when to expose himself on purpose in order to provoke his opponent to attack, and then use this moment for a counter-attack. Note also that a fight would sometimes end with the two men on the ground.

A *hoplomachus* and a *thraex* lacked large shields, but to make up for it their legs were fairly well protected. Armed with a spear, a *hoplomachus* naturally tried to fight at a longer, safer distance. Should his opponent (the *myrmillo*) manage to force him into close combat, his spear was no longer practical and the *hoplomachus* would drop it and switch to using his dagger with his right hand. A *thraex* had no such choice in close combat with a *myrmillo*, although a *sica* probably gave him certain advantages. The curved blade of a *sica* meant a gladiator could deliver thrusts round a shield or hook the opponent's shield aside (a *sica* with a broken blade was particularly good for this manoeuvre).

The *eques* had the least amount of protective armament of all the gladiators who carried a shield. A moderately small, round shield and the absence of greaves made him badly vulnerable. It is difficult to tell how a duel between two mounted *equites* played out – there are very few images showing this phase of fighting. We can only presume that the combat consisted of fast clashes, with both adversaries galloping at full speed. Then, after one of them fell down from his horse, or else at a signal given by the umpire, the *equites* switched to fighting on foot. Combat between a mounted and dismounted *equites* might have been forbidden, as no image represents such an action. Fighting dismounted, they had to move with great dynamism, constantly warding off the opponent's weapon with a shield.

Combat between a *retiarius* and a *secutor* is worth special analysis. A *retiarius* had nothing to rely upon but his own mobility and manoeuvrability. Close combat meant death for a *retiarius*, so he was perpetually on the move, now retreating, now circling around the *secutor*, choosing the moment either to throw the net upon him or thrust at him with a trident. It was a rare achievement to throw a net in such a way that the adversary was unable to disentangle himself. More often, a net only temporarily interfered with the movements of the hand holding a sword or shield, but it could be sufficient for dealing a decisive blow with a trident. The main targets for an attack with a trident were the opponent's head, his sword arm and his legs. Although the *secutor's* head was protected with a close helmet, a powerful blow from a trident thrust with both hands could still be decisive or, at least, stun the opponent for a fraction of a second. Moreover, although the eye-apertures in the *secutor's* helmet were small, they were still big enough for the point of a trident to pierce through them – the resulting wound would certainly end the fight. By catching his opponent's sword between the points of his trident and then turning the trident round in his hands, a *retiarius* could attempt to wrench the sword out of the *secutor's* hands or, at any rate, trap it for a moment while striking a blow with his dagger. A *retiarus* could also trip a *secutor* by making a trident attack on the *secutor's* legs, or on the edge of his adversary's shield to force the *secutor* to expose himself to an attack with the net or dagger.

A *thraex* recognisable by its high greaves, small shield and a crest in the shape of a griffin's head. Note that the shield protects the gladiator from helmet to greaves. 1st century AD. (British Museum, London. Author's collection)

A *secutor*, by contrast, did all he could to engage his adversary in close combat, so he attacked constantly, holding his large shield in front of him. With his much heavier armament, and a close-fitting helmet that restricted breathing, the *secutor* was slow-moving and had to spare his strength. To avoid eye-directed attacks from the trident, the *secutor* attacked with his head bent down.

Some of what Romans thought of various types of gladiator and their ways of fighting can be derived from Artemidorus' *Oneirocritica* (The Interpretation of Dreams), written in the second half of the 2nd century:

> I have noticed more than once that this dream [a dream about a gladiatorial combat] foretokens a marriage to a woman similar to either the weapon you are fighting with or the opponent with whom you are fighting in your dream... So one who dreams about fighting with a *thraex* will take a rich and perfidious wife who likes to have the upper hand in all: rich — because a *thraex* is all covered with armour, perfidious — because he fights with a curved dagger, and having the upper hand — because he is on the offensive. One fighting ... with silver weapons will marry a beautiful wife, not very rich, loyal, economical and pliable — because this fighter is in retreat, covered with armour, and his weapon is more beautiful than that of the first. One fighting with a *secutor* will have a beautiful and rich wife, but priding herself on her richness and so treating her husband slightingly, and the cause of many misfortunes because a *secutor* is always persecuting. One fighting in his dream with a *retiarius* will take a poor wife, passionate, licentious, readily giving herself to whoever so desires. A mounted fighter means that the wife will be rich, noble, but without brightness of mind. A charioteer means an idle and stupid wife; a *provocator* — a beautiful and nice, but greedy and passionate one; a gladiator with two swords or with a curved crescent — a poisoner or another perfidious and ugly woman.[181]

As we can see, Romans held the *thraex* and *secutor* as their favourites, looked down upon the *retiarius* with contempt, and held the *dimachaerus* and *arbelas* as the most insidious fighters.

CHAPTER V
AMPHITHEATRES

HISTORY

It is well known that gladiatorial contests took place in amphitheatres, as a rule, yet the structure itself appeared much earlier than the term. The first amphitheatres were built in Campania, where the idea of gladiatorial fights was conceived and originally put into practice. The main gladiator training centre remained here throughout the existence of the Republic. The most ancient surviving amphitheatre is in Pompeii, dating from 70 BC. In the dedication, the building is described as a *spectacula*, probably the term for amphitheatres at that time. The term *amphitheatrum* (amphitheatre) seems to have been born in Rome in the mid-1st century BC. It was first mentioned by Vitruvius around the 30s BC.[182] A later reference to it in Augustus' official papers shows that the word 'amphitheatre' was generally accepted.[183]

In Rome, the first amphitheatres were built in the mid-1st century BC, when two wooden buildings dedicated to *munera* were erected to replace the Forum used earlier for gladiatorial combat. The first was built by Gaius Scribonius Curio for the games in honour of his deceased father (52 BC). According to Plinius Secundus: 'He built two spacious wooden theatres next to each other, each balancing on a rotary mechanism. Ante-meridiem games were held in both theatres, each looking a different way so that the performances did not hamper each other. Then they were suddenly rotated to face each other, their ends joined forming an amphitheatre, where Curio arranged gladiatorial fights.'[184] Thus the amphitheatre consisted of two wooden theatres, each capable of rotating round a vertical axis. Joined together they formed a unitary amphitheatre. Owing to its construction, the building could

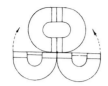

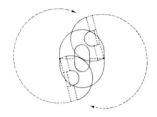

Two possible structures of Scribonius Curio's building. (Vladimir Golubev

be used for theatrical performances or gladiatorial games. One can only wonder at the complex mechanism setting in motion two theatres full of people. The axis soon became worn down and the structure functioned only as static amphitheatre. For a long time the two-theatre structure was in doubt among scholars, but descriptions given of amphitheatres by various ancient authors confirm that the term originated from the joining of theatres.[185]

The whereabouts of Curio's amphitheatre, or Julius Caesar's amphitheatre built in 46 BC, is unknown. The latter was most probably on the Campus Martius, together with all the later amphitheatres. The first amphitheatre made of stone, that of Statilius Taurus, was built in 29 BC. It must have had many wooden parts, as it was completely destroyed by the fire of AD 64. Nevertheless, wooden amphitheatres continued to be built alongside stone ones, and some experienced catastrophic structural failure. The amphitheatre built in 27 BC at Fidena was raised by an emancipated slave, Atilius. Limited in means, and either wishing to economise or just by mistake, he laid the foundation on unstable soil. A crowded amphitheatre crashed down during a performance, burying a great many people under the debris. Over 20,000 people were killed and the number of those injured reached 50,000. The Senate responded by passing a resolution forbidding the staging of gladiatorial games by those whose fortune was less than 400,000 sesterces, as well as prohibiting the erection of an amphitheatre without preliminary examination of the soil.[186]

By the turn of the millennium, Statilius Taurus' amphitheatre seems to have become inadequate to cope with the demands of the games. Many games were celebrated in other places. August and Caligula preferred the Saepta, a fenced place in the Campus Martius used for voting in the people's assembly. By 26 BC, the Saepta was enclosed in a marble wall with porticoes. Caligula began to build a new amphitheatre, but it was left unfinished.[187] Nero did not use Taurus' amphitheatre either; he erected a huge wooden structure in the Campus Martius.[188] Its raising took only one year, and in AD 57 it was opened, its inside decor abounding in gold and ivory. A few years later it perished in the famous fire of 64.

In 80 the Colosseum was opened in Rome to become the greatest amphitheatre in the world. The erection of this grandiose edifice began in 69 under Vespasian. His son Titus finished the construction and conducted the first games there. But it was only under Domitian that the construction of the amphitheatre was fully completed: he added four barracks for gladiators, an armoury, a hospital, *spoliarium* (mortuary), and barracks for the sailors of the fleet of Misenum, who operated the *velarium* awning (see below). All of these three emperors were of the Flavian dynasty;

therefore the official name of the construction was the Flavian Amphitheatre, although people later called it the Colosseum.[189] Next to the amphitheatre stood a 35m-high statue of Nero, which was then turned into the statue of Sola, God of the Sun, after Nero was overthrown and committed suicide. People used to call the huge statue 'colossus', hence the name of the amphitheatre.

From the beginning of the new era, amphitheatres were built all over the empire. The building programme became particularly intensive in the 2nd century. To date a total of 186 amphitheatres have been discovered, although there were undoubtedly more. In the provinces they were often smaller copies of the Colosseum. So-called 'military amphitheatres' were frequently built on the sites of stationary legionary camps, or nearby.[190] They were also used for meetings or shows, but in the first place for gladiatorial combat, which enhanced morale and inspired bravery and courage in soldiers.

Across the full extent of the empire, however, dedicated amphitheatres were relatively scarce and many gladiatorial games and *venatio* were staged in buildings meant for various other activities. Thus, the Hellenistic East knew only a few amphitheatres proper, but gladiatorial contests were by no means rare. Most such shows took place in theatres and stadiums, which were sometimes provided with specific additional security devices, such as higher walls around the *podium* to protect the public from wild animals. In Athens, for want of an amphitheatre, gladiators often fought in the famous Dionysus theatre near the Acropolis.[191]

Roman amphitheatre in Caerleon. It is the only fully excavated amphitheatre in the United Kingdom, and an excellent example of a military amphitheatre. Built AD 90, it has a 56×41m arena dug into the ground. The encircling embankment was made from the dug-up earth and faced with stone. A 9-high timber superstructure crowned the embankment and held seating. The amphitheatre housed about 6,000 spectators, which little outnumbered a legion. It was not only used for gladiatorial games and *venatio* but also for legionaries' parades and training. (Author's collection)

In Gallia some buildings were a hybrid of a theatre and amphitheatre. There were various types: some looked more like theatres, others like amphitheatres. Some combined the semicircular shape of a theatre with the elliptical arena of an amphitheatre, others had the appearance of a classical amphitheatre with an added theatre stage. These structures are more often discovered in the north of France, especially in Normandy. They are not seen in the south of France, where Roman influence was particularly strong. So it is rather a matter of local traditions in Gallo-Roman architecture than economy.[192]

In the Middle Ages, amphitheatres were often used as dwelling places by the dregs of society, or they were sometimes converted into fortresses by building additional towers. Many amphitheatres became objects of superstition and legends, or were popular locations for duels. The fate of the Colosseum is the best example of such a transformation in purpose: the structure was a witness to many historical events long after gladiatorial games were no longer celebrated there (see below for a more detailed history of the Colosseum).

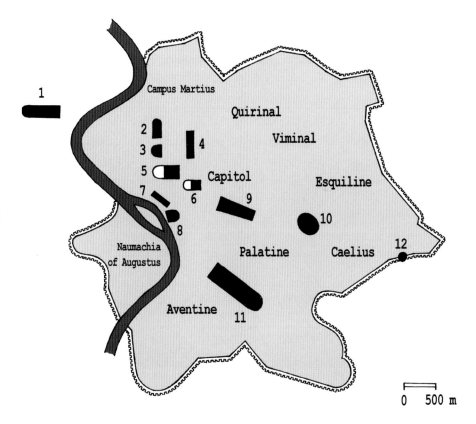

A map of Imperial Rome with circuses, theatres, amphitheatres and Saepta marked on it.
1 Circus of Caligula
2 Stadium of Domitian
3 Odeion of Domitian
4 Saepta Julia
5 Theatre of Pompey
6 Theatre of Balbus
7 Circus Flaminius
8 Theatre of Marcellus
9 Forum Romanum
10 Colosseum
11 Circus Maximus
12 Amphitheatrum Castrense
(Vladimir Golubev)

CONSTRUCTION

An amphitheatre was not always a detached building – only big, rich cities could afford one of those. Many amphitheatres were temporary constructions. For the sake of economy, amphitheatres were sometimes built on a hill slope or sunk deep in the ground, with earthen banks for tribunes made from the dug-out earth. The slope of a hill or the bank was shaped and rows of seats were cut into it; they were later faced with stone. This method saved considerable time, money and labour, particularly because there wasn't the requirement for the strong foundation necessary for a detached stone structure.

With the passage of time, the outside appearance of amphitheatres changed. For instance, the external staircases providing public access into earlier amphitheatres, like the one in Pompeii, were later taken inside, and the façade was adorned with arches, semi-columns and statues. We see these changes in many amphitheatres erected at the turn of the Republican and Imperial eras and later: the Colosseum in Rome and those in El Djem, Verona, Pula, Nimes and other places.

The arena (Latin *arena* meaning 'sand') of an amphitheatre was an elliptically shaped surface about 65–80m by 35–50m, covered with sand.[193] Such a large arena was not needed for gladiatorial combat, which normally were between unmounted combatants; it was, however, necessary for a *pompa* or *venatio*. The arena in most amphitheatres was not directly on the ground, but set on a wooden platform. Underneath the platform was a complex of cells and passages called *hypogeum*. It comprised stores of scenery and weapons, dressing rooms, premises for wild animals and the serving staff, as well as lifts for quickly bringing the performers up onto the stage (for the construction of the lifts see below, in the description of the Colosseum). Besides the *hypogeum*, a row of outbuildings, some with exits into the arena, stretched behind the high *podium* wall. (The *podium* was the first row of seats in the amphitheatre earmarked for the most notable spectators.) This gallery around the arena was called the *carcer*. It was generally used for auxiliary purposes, but it functioned as a *hypogeum* where the amphitheatre had no underground floor.

Under Caligula and Nero, the arena was particularly colourful at gala games: the sand in the arena was strewed with 'vermilion and chrysolite' so that the arena acquired a red or green colour.[194] The colours displayed the preferences of the two parties of chariot fans in the circus – the Reds and the Greens. For mythological scenes, wild animal hunting or dramatized executions, the arena was sometimes turned into a landscape with mountains, trees or other structures. Some amphitheatres, including the Colosseum before the *hypogeum* was built, had special

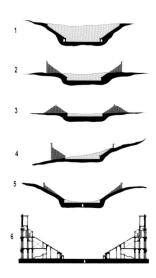

Types of amphitheatre: 1. Fully dug out in the ground. These amphitheatres were too labour-consuming and unpresentable and as such, were rarely found. 2. The arena and part of the tribunes lay below the surface level. 3. Only the arena was below the surface level. The embankments under the tribunes were erected with the earth dug up in making the arena. 4. The amphitheatre was 'stuck' to the slope of a hill. 5. The amphitheatre was made in a ravine between two hills. 6. The amphitheatre was a detached building standing apart from other structures. (Artist Vladimir Golubev)

Theatre in Hierapolis, Asia Minor. Amphitheatres were rarely built in the East of the Roman Empire. They preferred to give gladiatorial games and *venatio* in theatres or stadiums here. Numerous tombstones of gladiators discovered in the northern necropolis of the city show that gladiatorial games were often organised in this very theatre in Hierapolis. (Author's collection)

pools under the arena, which could be filled with water. During an ordinary show they were usually covered with a wooden platform. The pools were designed for performances of mythological stories and for chasing sea or river 'monsters' (crocodiles or hippopotami). A mini-*naumachia* was occasionally arranged, with small boats and ship models taking part. The arena was, however, too small for real *naumachia*, so the latter took place on a natural or artificial lake.

An arena was surrounded with a high wall (2.2–4m high) to protect the public from the beasts and gladiators.[195] However some big cats were capable of clearing this hurdle. So when they took part in the show, the height of the *podium* wall was increased with a tight net, or poles with a net stretched between them were put around the arena at a distance about 2–4m from the wall. The latter method was preferable, as it excluded both the possibility of an animal approaching as close as the *podium* wall and any activity taking place straight under the *podium* wall, where some of the spectators could miss it. An awning called a *velarium* was also stretched over the tribunes of the amphitheatre for protection against bad weather or bright sun. The *velarium* consisted of strips of cloth fixed on masts and was manipulated by professional sailors according to the position of the sun.

Seats in the amphitheatre (known as *loca* or *cavea*) were arranged to underline the social hierarchy. At the games of 194 BC, senators received seats separated from ordinary people for the first time. At the time this policy gave birth to numerous vigorous debates: some supported the idea, others criticized it furiously, accusing the senators of arrogance. In the end, Scipio Africanus himself, the author of the innovation, took the side of the latter.[196] However, the division of seats according to social position does not seem to have been repealed. Moreover, in 87 BC a special decree determined the first 14 rows in the theatres as the seats for equestrians.[197]

Despite these decrees, people did not feel too shy in choosing their own seats and until the end of the 1st century BC they sat in a fairly haphazard manner. A senator from Puteoli is known to have found no vacant seat to watch the show, and not a single person offered him one. The grudge born by the senator gave Augustus cause to introduce a well-defined division of seats at social performances. The first row was all for senators, the next 14 were left for equestrians. The regulations also provided fixed seats for soldiers, family citizens, non-Romans, youths and (separately) their tutors. Citizens wearing dark cloaks were forbidden to take seats in the middle. Women were only allowed to watch gladiatorial combat from the

This fresco represents a bloody quarrel between the natives of Pompeii and spectators from Nuceria. This scene took place in AD 59 in the Pompeian amphitheatre, which was closed for ten years as a consequence. This is one of the rare pictures of an amphitheatre where a *velarium* protecting the spectators from the sun and rain is clearly visible. (Museo Archeologico Nazionale, Napoli)

very upper seats (previously they used to sit together with men), while at athletic competitions they were forbidden to appear at all (mainly because athletes and boxers usually came out naked). Only women of the emperor's family and Vestals (Vestal Virgins) were allowed to watch gladiatorial combat from the first rows.[198]

Augustus was inexorable where his innovations were concerned: when spectators of pontifical games demanded boxing matches, the emperor postponed the competition until the next morning and declared that women must not appear before midday.[199] The decrees were valid across the entire territory of the Roman Empire, illustrated by numerous inscriptions that can still be seen in amphitheatres. It is curious that the seats reserved for each category of citizen were usually indicated by the space they occupied.[200] The emperor's box was generally in the centre of one of the long sides (at its crossing point with the shortest axis of the arena). Exactly opposite the emperor's box was a box for the members of the city council and the organizer of the games.

The structure of an amphitheatre was calculated so as to offer the spectators the best view of the arena – a distance of less than 60m from the spectator to the arena was considered optimal, although this was not always possible in big amphitheatres. In the Colosseum, for instance, the distance between the gallery and the arena reached 75m in some places. Acoustics were an even greater problem.

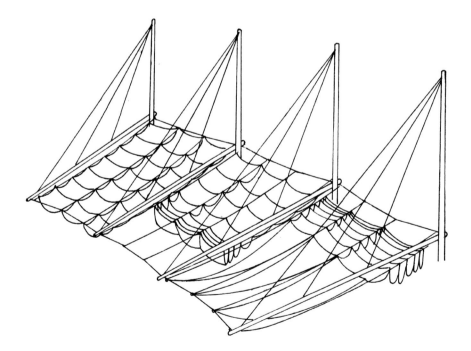

Velarium, an awning protecting spectators in the amphitheatre from hot sun or nasty weather. It was manipulated by specially recruited sailors. (Vladimir Golubev)

The sounds of music obviously could not beat the cries of active participants, the shouts and noise from the tribunes and the roar of the animals. Announcers' words were hardly audible in the upper rows.

In 2000, a modern performance that included the participation of horses was given in the Colosseum, offering an opportunity to assess the building's acoustic and visual potential. The experiment showed that only senatorial and equestrian-class seats offered visibility and audibility. For those sitting above, the performance was nothing but an alternation of bright spots. Spectators in those rows could only follow separate fights in the arena with great difficulty, and participated in the events chiefly through emotions, yielding to the general mood of the crowd. This situation explains the bright clothes and magnificent armour worn by gladiators, as it was only by them that the public in the gallery could tell one combatant from another. It also turned out in the course of the experiment that people working in the *hypogeum* probably had to communicate with the help of gestures: the rumble from dozens of people and animals on the arena floor was so deafening that even words uttered at a close distance were practically inaudible. Labour conditions in the *hypogeum* were aggravated by sand percolating down through the cracks of the wooden platform of the arena.[201]

Gladiators pictured on lamps and medallions. A whole branch of decorative industry was engaged in producing such household articles, for which gladiators were common subjects. (Römisch-Germanisches Museum, Köln. Author's collection)

A folding knife and its replica, 3rd century AD. The hilt of knife is moulded in the figure of a secutor. (British Museum, London. Author's collection)

Spartacus' insurrection revealed the great danger represented by gladiators. It was for protection from gladiators and to some extent from wild animals that a large number of soldiers were placed all about an amphitheatre. Also for security, it was only in the arena that weapons were handed to slave gladiators or criminals. At the same time, voluntary gladiators (*auctoratus*) must have been deemed harmless – the excavations in Pompeii revealed that they were neither disarmed nor kept in seclusion or hidden from the public.

It was also the duty of soldiers in the amphitheatre to stop disorder caused by fans. In 59 BC, a mob of fans in Pompeii flew into such a riotous temper that the amphitheatre was then closed for the next ten years:

> A trifling beginning led to frightful bloodshed between the inhabitants of Nuceria and Pompeii, at a gladiatorial show exhibited by Livineius Regulus… With the unruly spirit of townsfolk, they began with abusive language of each other; then they took up stones and at last weapons, the advantage resting with the populace of Pompeii, where the show was being exhibited. And so there were brought to Rome a number of the people of Nuceria, with their bodies mutilated by wounds, and many lamented the deaths of children or of parents.[202]

During a game, various souvenirs were sold inside the amphitheatre and nearby. A whole branch of decorative industry produced numerous mirrors, vessels, lamps, knife handles and other objects of art, engraved with the images of heroes of the arena and the most thrilling scenes of combat.

FAMOUS AMPHITHEATRES

The Colosseum is rightfully regarded as the biggest and most famous amphitheatre. It was built on the site that had once been occupied by a part of Nero's Domus Aurea (Golden House). The place was probably chosen by the Emperor Vespasian on the basis of ideological considerations, part of a programme of destruction of all memorials erected by the odious Nero. The money for the construction of the Colosseum was drawn from the booty taken during the Jewish War, and the labourers were mainly Jewish slaves. Travertine used for the construction was obtained from a quarry about 30km from Rome – the quarry was connected with Rome by a road built by 30,000 Jews labouring along the distance in two unbroken lines.[203] In AD 70, the Roman Army led by the future emperor Titus had seized

Jerusalem and plundered the famous Solomon's Temple. Ten years later, in 80, when opening the Colosseum, Emperor Titus organized magnificent 100-day celebrations, including *naumachia*, *munera* and *venatio*.

Like all classical amphitheatres, the Colosseum has an oval shape. It occupies a 188×156m site (the longest and the shortest diameters of the ellipse respectfully);

A general view and a cutaway view of a model reconstruction of the Flavian Amphitheatre. Reconstructed by Carlo Lucangeli and Paolo Dalbono. (Archivio della Soprintendenza Archeologica, Rome)

the arena is 76×44m. The Colosseum was the highest building in ancient Rome – the height of its outer walls exceeded 52m. The walls consisted of four tiers: the first three had open corridors with 80 arches, the fourth was closed, with light penetrating into it through windows. The first tier was decorated with Doric semi-columns, the second with Ionic, and the third with Corinthian, while the fourth tier was broken up with Corinthian pilasters. Marble statues stood in every arch of the second and third tiers. Along the top of the wall there were 240 wooden masts on which a *velarium* was fastened. The awning could be of various colours: yellow, red, light blue, brown or purple. The entire building was enclosed in a 1.75m-high wall, and so the amphitheatre found itself surrounded with a passage as wide as 17.6m.

The Flavian Amphitheatre could be entered through all the 80 arches of the lower tier, but common people could only use 68 of them – another six arches were earmarked for nobility and the remaining six were for the participants in the games. The entrance for the emperor was on the northern side. The total number of seats, according to contemporary calculations, reached 87,000; however, according to modern calculations it varies between 50,000 and 73,000. The system of entrances and exits allowed all the spectators to leave the amphitheatre in less than five minutes.[204]

Citizens of each social class had assigned seats, with separate passages leading to them. Equestrian-class citizens and senators could take their seats and leave them without coming into contact with common people. The seats were divided into three sectors, partitioned by low walls (*baltei*). The first section (*ima cavea* or *podium*), the nearest to the arena and consisting of four tiers, was occupied by senators and their families as well as Vestals. The emperor's box was also to be found here; it does not survive, though, so we can only guess at its splendour. Today, inscriptions with the names of senators can still be seen beside the marble seats of this sector.[205] It was separated from other seats in the amphitheatre by the *balteus* wall decorated with mosaics. The second sector (*maenianum primum*) counted eight tiers and was assigned for the equestrian class. Finally, the third sector (*maenianum summum in ligneis*), the most capacious and remote from the arena, was for plebeians and women. There was an open gallery on top, where people could stand to watch the performance.

The reconstruction of a section of seating in the eastern sector of the Colosseum, made in the course of restoration work in 1938/39, is now considered incorrect. The way the *podium* wall and the slope of the *podium* were reconstructed has garnered the strongest criticism. The latest research shows that the slope of the *podium* must have been 19 degrees, not 30 degrees as it was made in the course of the reconstruction work. The slope of 30 degrees was only characteristic of the other seats of the amphitheatre.[206]

Recent research has also revealed a clever sewerage system in the Colosseum. It ensured the functioning of numerous toilets scattered about the entire building, making possible the accommodation of such a mass of people. Moreover, water was brought up through special tubes to the fountains in the covered galleries between the second and third sectors of the amphitheatre.

Spectators occupied their seats strictly according to the 'tickets' – special tablets, a great number of which have been found. Some of them offer detailed information; for example, 'Cun VI In[feriori] [gradu decimo] VIII', which meant tier 6, row 10, seat 8. Others only indicate the type of the show for which the 'ticket' was valid, for instance 'LUD (I)' – Games (I), or 'DIES VENAT[ionis]' – *venatio* days.[207] In the latter case, spectators knew beforehand what seats to occupy. Every arch in the Colosseum carried an inscription detailing to which seats the entrance led, so that the public could quickly take their place.

The arena of the Colosseum was a wooden platform covered with sand. At first, when it was constructed, the architects envisaged the possibility of filling the arena

Flavian Amphitheatre. The arena lacks its planking so the whole complex of the underground rooms (*hypogeum*) is clearly seen. (Topfoto)

with water from the nearest reservoirs on the Caelian Hill. However, about the mid-2nd century, a big *hypogeum* complex was built underneath the arena, now visible as the arena has been deprived of the platform.[208] The *hypogeum* of the Colosseum is divided into several corridors. Rather curious is the system of elevators that brought people, animals and decorations up onto the arena. In different corridors, and evidently at different times, there existed three different structures of elevators.

So-called corridor B had 28 elevators lifting cages sized 1.6×1.4×1.1m (length, width and height) up to the arena. Because of the limited height of the cages, these elevators were probably used for lifting animals (wolves, wild boars, medium-size felines and so on), not people. An elevator was brought into operation by windlasses on two tiers, with four men on each tier. Therefore, 224 men were needed to work all the elevators of the corridor. The floors of the elevators could not be raised to the level of the arena, on account of the height of the cages. As a solution, a part of the arena platform was moved downward to the level of the cage floor. When the cage door was opened, the animals went up an inclined plane to the arena.

In the course of a rebuilding of the *hypogeum*, the elevators in corridor B were taken away. New elevators, installed in corridors E and G were to be used instead. These were 0.9×1.3–1.4m platforms moving upward almost to the level of the arena. A windlass with ropes running through rollers lifted the elevator. At the same time, a section of the arena platform was drawn away so that people or animals could step straight into the arena. There were 60 elevators of this structure in the Colosseum: 20 in corridor E (10 on the northern side and 10 on the southern) and 40 in corridor G (20 on the northern side and 20 on the southern).

The elevators in corridors H and F had a different construction. There were 20 large mobile platforms here, each 4×5m. In the closed position they formed a part of the arena platform. When opened, they slid downward along special guides inclined at 30 degrees. They were moved upward by a system of windlasses.

Shown here is a reconstruction of the system of lifts in corridor B of the *hypogeum* in the Colosseum. After H-J. Beste. (Artist Vladimir Golubev)

These elevators were used for bringing up scenery and people (the people were needed to arrange the scenery in the arena). Gladiators may have used these elevators, too; the construction, however, prevented an impressive appearance into the arena: the movement of the elevators was far from smooth, so people had to hold on tightly.

Along the Colosseum's main axis there were two exits leading to the arena – Porta Triumphalis and Porta Libitinensis. Through the first gate gladiators came out onto the arena, while through the second their dead bodies were taken away. The very last performance (*venatio*) in the Flavian Amphitheatre took place in 523.

As well as the Colosseum, there was another amphitheatre in Rome, known as the Castrense Amphitheatre. Built around the early 3rd century, it was used by Elagabalus for watching gladiatorial combat and *venatio* in the company of a close circle of his retainers – this extremely corrupt emperor particularly enjoyed watching a game before having a meal. The amphitheatre was comparatively small,

Here we can see a reconstruction of a system of lifts in corridor E of the *hypogeum* in the Colosseum. After H-J. Beste. (Artist Vladimir Golubev)

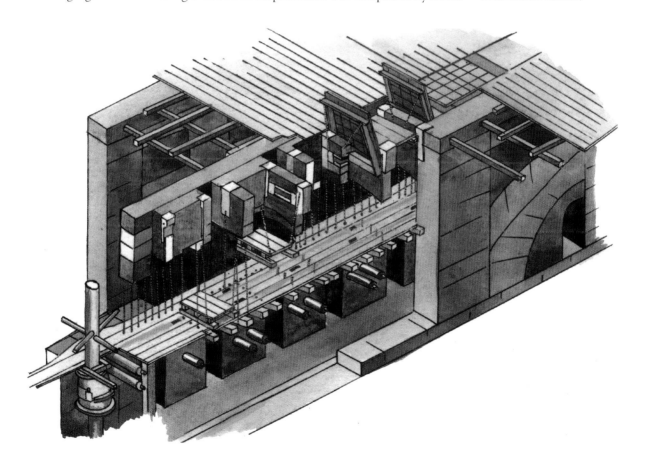

with a 38×25m arena, and supposedly could not house more than 3,500 spectators. Elagabalus' successor, Alexander Severus (r. 222–235), disliked the amphitheatre and ignored it; under Aurelian (r. 270–275) the amphitheatre was included into the city's fortifications. The impressive ruins of this amphitheatre, partly absorbed by the Aurelian Wall, can still be seen today. After Elagabalus' death, the amphitheatre seems to have only served as a *vivarium* – a place where animals for *venatio* were kept. It was once mistakenly believed that the amphitheatre had been built and used for praetorian training and it is sometimes called a 'camp' or 'military' amphitheatre.[209]

In the Middle Ages, the Colosseum witnessed many gruesome scenes. Turned into a fortress during the internecine wars of the 13th century, it was then seized by Saracens, who took up residence. After their withdrawal, the Colosseum was partly destroyed to prevent it being turned into a citadel again. It housed a great *corrida* and was used for several mystery plays. It then became a hospital, and then a factory. All through the Middle Ages, the Colosseum, as a place where many Christian martyrs had been put to death, was an object of pilgrimage. The money collected by pilgrims proved enough to build a church on the *podium*; the church was entrusted to an anchorite, who also had the right to lease the grass growing in the arena. By contrast, the amphitheatre gained ill fame in medieval Rome. Orgies took place here, and numerous adventurers searched the place for ancient treasures. Moreover, a great many homeless people found shelter there, turning some parts of the Colosseum into throngs of hovels.[210]

The Colosseum gradually decayed – less than half of it survives, but the ruins still produce a great impression. Stones from the Colosseum were used for erecting three buildings – the Pope's office, and the Venetian and Farnese palaces. Today the 186 surviving amphitheatres are scattered about the territory of the former Roman Empire. Apart from the Colosseum, well-preserved amphitheatres are to be found in Italy at Pompeii, Pozzuoli, Capua and Verona; in France at Arles and Nimes; in Croatia at Pula; and in Tunisia at El Djem.

The structure of the amphitheatre in Pompeii differs from that of the Colosseum. It is half-embedded in the ground, and spectators entered it from above, through the passageway that surrounded the amphitheatre and was fed by four staircases. The size of the amphitheatre is 136×104m, and its 35 rows had enough room for 20,000 spectators.

The amphitheatre in Capua is famous because Spartacus, who stirred up a slave rebellion in 73 BC, fought in gladiatorial combats there. In his time the amphitheatre looked different, though, as at the end of the 1st century AD it was rebuilt following the pattern of the Colosseum. It is the second largest amphitheatre in Italy, and housed up to 60,000 spectators. Like the Flavian Amphitheatre, it was decorated with arches and statues.

In the amphitheatre at Verona, the seats are in good condition, but only a few bays are left of the outer wall. In Pula, on the contrary, the impressive outer wall is well preserved, while practically nothing is left of the *cavea* seats in the amphitheatre, once capable of holding 22,000 spectators. The amphitheatre in Nimes, dating from Augustus' rule, is 132×101m, with the arena as large as 69×39m. This amphitheatre is in excellent condition, despite all the peripeteia of fortune in its history. First the Visigoths turned it into a fortress surrounded by a ditch and strengthened with two towers (the towers were pulled down early in the 19th century). Then the Saracens made it their fortress, but they were driven out by the leader of the Franks, Charles Martel. After that the amphitheatre became a refuge for a military order, and then for the paupers of the city of Nimes. Finally, in 1533, Francis I visited it and went

into such raptures at the sight of this tremendous ancient building that he would crawl on all fours among the stones, trying to make out the ancient inscriptions. He then ordered that all the hovels in the amphitheatre be pulled down.

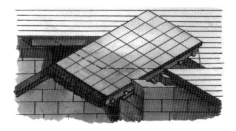

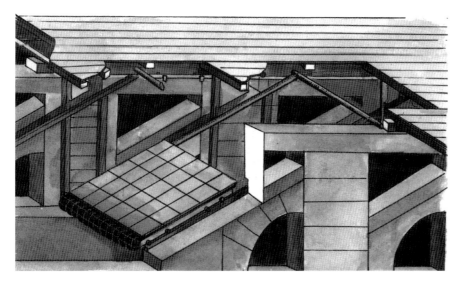

Here is a reconstruction of a system of lifts in corridor H of the *hypogeum* in the Colosseum. After H-J. Beste. (Artist Vladimir Golubev)

The Arles amphitheatre was built about half a century later than that of Nimes, and is about the same size (136×108m, with a 69×39m large arena) as the latter. Their constructions are so much alike that they were probably erected by the same architect or, at least, by architects of the same school. The amphitheatre housed 25,000 spectators. Like other amphitheatres, it was turned into a fortress in the 12th century, but three of the original four square towers

Presented here are two views of the famous amphitheatre in El Djem, which was a replica of the Roman Colosseum, built late 2nd or early 3rd century AD. (Author's collection)

survive. In the Middle Ages the amphitheatre of Arles was inhabited by 2,000 people speaking many different dialects.[211]

The first amphitheatre to appear in El Djem (El Jem, former Thysdrus) was constructed over 2,000 years ago. It was probably built as far back as the mid-1st century BC by immigrants from Campania or Etruria, who came to Africa together with Caesar. It was a primitive structure dug out of the slopes of a hill, without a trace of masonry. In the 1st century AD another amphitheatre was erected in El Djem. It was also situated on the slope of a hill, but the seats for spectators, partitioned into special sectors, were made from stone. The late 2nd or early 3rd century saw construction begin on a more famous amphitheatre, one which strongly resembled the Roman Colosseum (the Colosseum was probably used as a model). According to popular belief, the third amphitheatre in Thysdrus owed its birth to Emperor Gordian III. In 238 an insurrection in Africa resulted in the proclamation of Gordian I of Thysdrus as Roman Emperor, but he was dead before a month of his rule was over. After taking the throne, his grandson Gordian III presented his native city with a splendid amphitheatre. It was 148m long and 122m wide. The three tiers with arcades rose 39m high. The arena was 64m long and had a *hypogeum* underneath consisting of two galleries with cells for animals and gladiators. The amphitheatre is supposed to have housed 27,000 people.[212] In the Middle Ages, it often served as a fortress. Here the local population sought shelter from the assault of the Vandals in 430 and from the Arabs in 647. The last time the amphitheatre

The eldest of the two surviving amphitheatres in El Djem. Spectators' seats were partitioned into special stone sectors. 1st century AD. (Author's collection)

The *hypogeum* of the amphitheatre in El Djem. In this half-dark underground floor people and animals awaited their entrance onto the arena. Two kinds of chambers flanked the central passage: open cells, with traces of runners, and closed rooms with a door and a window. The former must have been for cages with animals, the latter – for gladiators or *noxii*. (Author's collection)

was used as a fortress was in 1695, when Mohammed Bey smashed a large breach in its walls to drive out the adherents of Ali Bey.

A few other amphitheatres are worth mentioning. The amphitheatre of Casinum (near modern Cassino, Italy) has a round, not elliptic, arena. In Sutrium (or Sutri, Italy) spectators' seats, corridors and the arena are carved right into the rock. No traces of an amphitheatre in Ostia – mentioned in some sources – have been found so far. The amphitheatre in Catania (Sicily) was buried under a layer of lava. An amphitheatre has been revealed in a relatively small building in Emerita (modern Mérida, Spain). The arena of the amphitheatre in ancient Caesarea (Mauretania) was 140×60m, which is considerably larger than the arena of the Colosseum.[213]

In addition to those mentioned above, amphitheatres have been revealed in Gortyna and Hierapytna on Crete; in Corinthus (Corinth) on the Peloponnese; in Aphrodisias, Comana, Cyzicus and Pergamum in Asia Minor; Alexandria in Egypt; Dura-Europos in Syria. A great many amphitheatres were concentrated in the Roman province of Africa, particularly where modern Tunisia is situated. Besides the amphitheatre in El Djem, 30 more amphitheatres are known to have existed there, although not all of them have yet been revealed.[214]

CHAPTER VI
ORGANIZING THE EVENTS

ORGANIZATION OF *MUNUS*

The organization of *munus* always cost a lot of money. *Munera* became particularly expensive in the 1st–2nd centuries, when people had developed a taste for such shows and demanded increasingly protracted performances with more and more pairs of gladiators and exotic animals involved. Officials forced by their position in society to stage luxurious games would often find themselves on the verge of complete financial ruin. An organizer of the games frequently fell victim to a greedy *lanista*, who asked for an exorbitant price to provide the combatants. The market price of a gladiator depended directly on the scale of the games. In the 2nd century, for instance, a first-class gladiator for a show that cost 30,000–60,000 sesterces would come to no more than 5,000 sesterces, but his price could fly up to 15,000 sesterces for a show that cost 200,000 sesterces or more.[215] Even the cheapest gladiator (a *gregarium*), who participated in mass battles, was as expensive as 1,000 to 3,000 sesterces.[216] Just for comparison: 500 sesterces would sustain a peasant family for a whole year.

Gladiatorial games were a powerful instrument for influencing the masses. Therefore, a number of acts regulating *munera* were passed by the Senate. For instance, an act was promulgated in 22 BC to the effect that any person wishing to organize games should obtain the approval of the Senate. Moreover, a man was not allowed to stage games more than twice a year, with the number of gladiators enlisted not exceeding 120.[217] During Tiberius' rule, the Senate decreed that a person whose property was valued at less than 400,000 sesterces (the equivalent of an average equestrian's property value) was forbidden from organizing a *munus*.[218] Marcus Aurelius issued regulations that imposed fixed prices on various expenditures connected with the organization of games, which would also hold in check the price of gladiator.[219]

First, the tax collected by the state from *lanistae* was abolished on the basis that 'imperial money should be clean'. This policy resulted in tradesmen lowering the prices of hired gladiators. Second, the upper limit for the price of gladiators was established according to the class of combatants and the cost of the games. The latter were separated into five classes, with the four upper classes obliged to enlist at least half of the combatants from the *gregarium* class. If a *lanista* an had insufficient number of gladiators of the lower class, he would make up for their shortage with gladiators of higher qualification, but rent them at a price not exceeding the maximum price of a *gregarium*. The application of Aurelius' regulations extended to big cities; the upper limit for the expenditures in small towns was established by averaging out the accounts for the games for the previous ten years.[220]

One could get round the regulations by specially appealing to the Senate or directly to the emperor. During Nero's time, for instance, Syracusans are known to have asked for the Senate's permission to exceed the number of gladiators.[221]

In Rome, the main organizer of the games (*editor*) in the Imperial period was certainly the emperor. In reality, the honour, or to be exact, responsibility for the organization of *munera* was laid on praetors under the emperors from Augustus to

Caligula, and later on quaestors. In the provinces, *munera* were to be organized by magistrates, who were allowed to spend a certain part of their revenue (depending on the wealthiness and size of a town or province) on annual performances.[222]

The organization of gladiatorial games cost less to the emperor than to a private person, as the former was less dependent on the market price of gladiators, who were supplied to him by imperial schools. In Rome alone there were as many as four imperial gladiatorial schools, and a considerable number of imperial schools were dispersed all over Italy and various provinces. Heads of schools in Rome were chosen from among the class of equestrians, while in other towns special procurators (*procuratores familiarum gladiatoriarum*) were appointed.[223] *Munera* held by a private person became more and more scarce in the empire, even in the provinces. Excessive expenditures and numerous restrictions made it an emperor's prerogative to appear as *editor* of a *munus*.

In the Imperial period the *munus* was organized following a strictly planned scheme. At first the *editor* made an agreement with a *lanista* stipulating, in detail, the number and qualification of gladiators he would like to acquire or lend. In case of a purchase, the *editor* paid a full market price for all the gladiators he bought. In case of a lease, he paid a full price only for the killed gladiators and a certain sum for the work performed by those who remained alive. Thus, the more gladiators who were killed, the greater the expenses of the *editor*. On the one hand, *editors* were not interested in frequent death sentences; on the other hand they had to pass such sentences from time to time lest the people judged them as miserly.

The next step was to attract public attention to the event. This was achieved by writing advertisements (*edicta muneris*) in red paint, as a rule, on the walls of buildings, on city gates and even on gravestones. Moreover, posters with such advertisements were carried about the city by special slaves, while public criers read them out loud in the squares. *Edicta muneris* usually contained the following information: the event which was to be honoured by the games, the *editor*'s name, the number of the pairs of gladiators and the name of their troupe (*familia gladiatoria*), a list of other entertainments in the programme (*venatio*, athletic competitions, execution of criminals), measures to be taken for the spectators' additional comfort (such as a sun-shading awning, the distribution of gifts, the spraying of aroma), the place and time of the performance. An opportunity to receive a gift was a great stimulus to attendance, attracting crowds of people to the amphitheatre. Among these gifts (*missilia*) there could be food, coins and coupons that entitled the holder to receive various things given free of charge. Even pearls and precious stones were

Opposite:
Dimachaerus, 2nd–3rd centuries AD. (Author's reconstruction, artist Vladimir Golubev)

given at the more luxurious performances. The spraying of aroma (*sparsio*) and a flower 'rain', offered also in circuses and theatres, were no less attractive to the public. In the stuffy atmosphere caused by a great concentration of masses of people, they brought freshness and a bit of comfort.

More than 80 such *edicta muneris* have been preserved on the walls of Pompeii, for example: 'Gladiators of edile Suettius Caerius will perform in Pompeii on May 31. Beast chasing will be organized under the awning in the amphitheatre.' Another states: 'Beast chasing will take place on August 28 – Felix fighting with bears.'

A *retiarius* and two *secutores* fighting for the platform in the 2nd–3rd centuries AD. (Author's reconstruction, artist Vladimir Golubev)

One or two days before the games, gladiators were displayed for public observation, an event that usually happened in the forum. A banquet for all the participants of the forthcoming performances (*cena libera*) was given on the eve of the games. Entrance was free, so any citizen could drop in and have a close look at the gladiators who were to fight in the arena the next day.

Choosing gladiatorial pairs (*compositio*) was no easy matter. It was possibly done by the *editor* on agreement with the *lanista* and the *doctores* (the gladiators' trainer in a gladiatorial school). However, not a single *edicta muneris* names the paired gladiators. It may mean that the pairs were composed at the last moment by way of casting lots in front of the spectators. In this case the sorting must have been held separately for each rank of gladiators, as every pair was to consist of more or less equally trained combatants, to prevent the disappointment of a swiftly ended fight. Therefore a novice would hardly be seen fighting against a veteran of the arena. There is, however, no rule without exception. A novice could occasionally prove so gifted that he dominated an acknowledged hero of the amphitheatre in the first combat. A surviving inscription in Pompeii informs us that a novice *myrmillo* Marcus Attilius defeated the veteran *thraex* Hilarus, who had been victorious 14 times. The latter was granted his life and he left the arena on foot. In his next combat, Marcus Attilius defeated the *thraex* Lucius Recius Felix, who had been engaged in 12 combats and each time received the victor's wreath. The defeated Lucius also left the arena alive. These victories over veterans cannot be explained by pure luck. Marcus Attilius was undoubtedly a very gifted fighter and had received excellent training.

ORGANIZATION OF *VENATIO*

An insight into all the difficulties involved in organising a *venatio* can be derived from the surviving letters of Quintus Aurelius Symmachus. In 393, having proposed himself as candidate to the post of quaestor, his son organised gladiatorial games. On the eve of the games, however, 29 Saxon prisoners, who were to appear in the arena, committed suicide. Only a few of the bears that had been bought were supplied in time, and even those few were hungry and tired when they arrived. Moreover, some of the animals had drowned in a shipwreck. It was only owing to the emperor, who partly compensated Quintus for the losses, that the situation was saved.

In 401 Quintus Aurelius Symmachus' son sought the office of praetor. This time, three years were to be spent on preparation for the games. It was necessary to obtain the emperor's permission to buy wild animals and also to hold the games in the Flavian Amphitheatre (the Colosseum); friends had to be contacted in provinces and asked to supply the beasts. At last, after three years of incessant effort, Symmachus succeeded in getting horses from Spain, dogs from Britain, bears from Italy and the northern and eastern districts of the Adriatic Sea, lions, leopards and antelopes from Africa and crocodiles from Egypt. All did not go off smoothly here either. Out of 16 horses supplied from Spain, five did not survive the trip and the rest died in Rome, never living to see the opening of the games.[224]

As we can see, the organization of the *venatio* in the Colosseum was no easy matter and one demanding great expenditure. Therefore, gladiatorial games in Rome were only given by emperors. The celebration offered by Quintus Aurelius Symmachus was the only known exception. In provinces, *venationes*, as well as *munera*, were organized by magistrates. Of course, they were arranged on a more modest scale than those displayed in Rome. For instance, lions and elephants, so dearly loved by the Romans, were absent as a rule, as emperors had settled a monopoly on these animals. Sometimes, however, it was possible to come to an agreement with the emperor and acquire them from the imperial menagerie – such usually occurred in the years when financial problems made it burdensome for an emperor to keep a great number of voracious animals. For instance, in 273, Emperor Aurelian gave out as presents 20 elephants and 200 various tamed animals of other species to relieve the burden the state had in feeding them.[225]

There were several African societies engaged in beast trading. Each society had its own name, number and symbol. The most famous of them were the Telegenii, operating under number III and with a symbol of a crescent on a pole. (The symbol came from the instrument designed to prick animals in the arena.) The Telegenii considered Dionysus their protector. There were also other societies: Pentasii, number IIIII, symbolized by a crown with five teeth; Tauresci, number II, symbolized by an ivy leaf; and Leontii, number IIII, symbolized by a millet stem, with Venus as protector.[226] As early as the Republican era there were animal markets in Africa and Asia where necessary beasts could be bought for a *venatio*. The animals here were divided into three categories: 1) exotic (usually only displayed to the public), 2) herbivorous and 3) beasts of prey.[227]

Any Roman citizen wishing to organize a *venatio* first had to send a formal application to the governor of the province where he wanted to buy animals. This official route was rarely chosen, however – most noble Romans preferred to count on personal contacts with the governor. The latter was only too happy to help his friends in the capital, hoping for their support in the future. In general, poaching of animals as well as acquiring them from both local inhabitants and local officials was forbidden; the governor regarded this as the organizer exceeding his authority. Such was the reason why, after taking the post of governor of Cilicia in 51 BC, Cicero refused to supply a friend in Rome with animals until he received an official application from him as the organizer of the games.[228]

CATCHING ANIMALS

Not only local hunters but soldiers as well were involved in catching animals. Frontier legions and legions located in 'wild' provinces included special detachments of hunters (*venatores*) engaged in catching beasts. For instance, soldiers of the 1st Legion of Minerva under the centurion's command are known to have caught about 50 bears during six months, and a soldier of the 30th Legion who

Part of a mosaic depicting the catching of a tiger with a help of a round mirror. Seeing its own reflection, the beast mistakes it for its own cub, and, rushing forward to save it, got into the trap. It dates from early 4th century AD. (Ancient Art and Architecture)

specialized in catching bears was even awarded the rank of a *ursarius legiones* (bear-hunter-legionary).[229] Hunter legionaries were exempt from everyday duties and training.

There were three main methods of catching animals. Mounted hunters could drive a beast of prey into a big cage, with a goat tied nearby as bait. The goat was sometimes tied behind the cage, or even on a special platform pulled inside the cage by a hunter. Hunters holding spears and shields stood on both sides of the cage, making a 'live' corridor. A hunter standing on the roof of the cage held its door open. When the animal went inside, he shut the door.

Pictured in this mosaic are members of various African corporations who are engaged in the delivery of animals for *venatio*. A representative of each corporation has a characteristic symbol: a crown with five teeth, an ivy leaf, a crescent on a pole, and others. (Musée National du Bardo, Tunis. Author's collection)

ANIMALS SUPPLIED FROM DIFFERENT COUNTRIES IN THE IMPERIAL PERIOD.	
Britannia	Deer, elks, dogs
Upper Egypt and Ethiopia	Giraffes, monkeys, antelopes
Gaul	Elks, wolves, bears
Germany	Bison
Egypt	Hippopotami, rhinoceroses, crocodiles, gazelles
India	Tigers, monkeys, wild asses
Spain and Dalmatia	Bears, fallow-deer, horses
Italy	Deer, wild boars, foxes, bears, hares, wolves and bulls
Crete	Wild goats
North Africa	Lions, leopards, antelopes, jackals, hyenas, gazelles, elephants
Phrygia and Mauritania	Wild asses

Another method also involved the use of a cage, but it was placed at the bottom of a pit. The pit was covered with branches of trees and twigs, and a bait was put on top. A lion or leopard jumped at the bait and fell into the pit. Here, an open cage with a piece of meat stood waiting for it. As soon as the beast was in the cage, the door was closed and the cage lifted to the surface. An enclosure surrounded by nets was used in the third method. Waving burning torches and rattling their shields, mounted hunters frightened animals into an area fenced with nets, where a net was thrown over each of them and they were driven into a cage.

The catching of a lioness with a cage. There is a wheeled platform in front of the cage, to which a goat is tied as bait. 4th century AD. (Carthaginian Museum, Tunis. Author's collecion)

139

There was an additional, and very cunning, method occasionally used to catch a big cat. The animal was lured with a round mirror in which it could see its own reflection. Taking the reflection for its young, the animal rushed forward to free it and found itself in a cage.[230] Lions may also have been caught by throwing a cloak over their heads — a lion was supposed to calm down when he could not see his adversary.[231] However these methods were only of minor importance. Taking lion or tiger cubs to be reared was a rare practice — it was an extremely dangerous enterprise that more than once cost hunters and horses their lives, as the parents rushed to defend their infants. If the hunters failed to disappear before a parent arrived, the cub had to be left behind.

Elephants were caught by driving them into camouflaged pits and shooting arrows at their legs. They could occasionally climb out however, raking up the earth with their feet or pulling themselves up and out with their trunks. One possibility is that tame elephants were used for catching wild ones — this was a very common method in India, but it is not clear if Romans used it in Africa. Bison were driven into a pit that had its bottom and sides covered with fresh, specially lubricated hides. Chased by mounted hunters, the animals slipped on the hides and rolled into the pit. It was in the pit that their taming began, when they were starved for several days. Nets and pits were helpful in catching bears, too, after they were driven out of their dens with the help of dogs.[232]

The most common way of driving herbivorous animals into a fenced enclosure was by using dogs. To lure a deer, a hunter could play the flute or tie a tame deer in a thicket and then hide and wait for the animal's cries to attract other creatures. Many animals were trapped or caught with lassos. Nets set up in shallow waters where animals came to water could also bring in a catch. Birds as well as crocodiles and big snakes were also caught in nets.[233]

Far-fetched methods of catching animals are sometimes found in the primary sources, as for instance, giving a panther wine mixed with water to drink, or laying a mixture of soot with pitch under a monkey's nose, provoking it to glue up its eyes with the sticky substance whereupon it was easily caught.[234]

Trapped animals were kept in a menagerie (*vivaria*). Some were sent to Rome or other big cities; some, however, were killed in amphitheatres situated on the territory of a military camp or in the neighbourhood. Intensive hunting of animals for *venatio* certainly had a dramatic impact on the fauna of North Africa: by the 4th century, elephants had become completely extinct in the region and once numerous felines sharply decreased in number.

TRANSPORTATION

Dangerous animals were transported in cages, which seem to have been different in structure from those used for catching the beasts in the first place. Some animals, for instance, wild boars, remained entangled for the whole journey in the net they had been caught in. Elephants and bulls were hobbled during transportation. Meanwhile, small or medium-sized herbivorous, such as ostriches, gazelles and so on, probably enjoyed considerable freedom on board a ship. Some images show them loaded on board with bare hands.

For short distances, caged animals were also carried by hand: two porters carried the cage on a pole that rested on their shoulders. For long distances, four-wheeled carts were used. Water transportation was always preferred – it was much simpler to transport animals on board a ship down a river or across the sea. The ships coming to Italy were unloaded in Ostia or Pozzuoli, from where the animals were taken to amphitheatres in Campania or Rome. From Ostia to Rome, ships with animals were usually pulled up the river Tiber by bulls, and frequently by people, too, who walked along the road specially built for it on the right-hand bank of the river.[235] The road from Pozzuoli to Rome was much longer, and the animals had to be transported by land.

It could take months to bring animals from far-off provinces to Rome. During that time many animals could die from illnesses or drown in a shipwreck, which meant a great loss of money for the organizer of the games. Responsibility for the safe transportation of animals, as well as for the proper functioning of imperial gladiatorial schools, lay with the procurators of provinces, while the maintenance of a caravan of animals on the road to Rome was the responsibility of the officials in the province through which it was passing.[236] The latter was a fairly onerous task, which is why the time of a caravan's stay in a town was usually restricted to a few days. Abuses occurred, though. For instance, in 417 a caravan was detained for three or four months in Hierapolis (Syria). Its billeting turned out to be so burdensome for the city that the governor of the province sent a protest to the emperor. The latter issued an edict forbidding caravans to stay in a town longer than seven days.[237]

In Rome, the *vivaria* must have been situated in the suburbs, as many animals were dangerous and their escape was not unknown.[238] There was even a law providing monetary compensation in case of any free Roman citizen's death, trauma or damage to his property (slaves included) caused by a runaway animal.[239] Imperial menageries were kept under close watch by Praetorian Guards, who as we know occasionally took part in *venatio*.[240] Animals were delivered to the amphitheatre on the eve of the games or early in the morning on the day of the *venatio*, as at night animals were calmer and the streets of the Eternal City were deserted.

Where the animals were kept until the performance remains uncertain. The cellars of the Colosseum were not spacious enough to house the hundreds of animals that sometimes participated simultaneously in the same *venatio*. Perhaps the beasts were gathered at the Ludus Matutinus (Morning School), which was situated near the Colosseum, in the vicinity of modern Via Claudia, and from there were brought to the amphitheatre via a special corridor.[241]

GLADIATORIAL SCHOOLS AND TRAINING

Model of ancient Rome, showing the Colosseum and the complex of Ludus Magnus, the gladiatorial school. (© Araldo de Luca / Corbis)

Gladiatorial schools (*ludi*) were private or imperial. The former were the province of private entrepreneurs. Proprietors of gladiatorial schools belonged to the senatorial class as a rule, while *lanistae* could be freeborn or freedmen, or even slaves. A *lanista* either bought or employed suitable people, trained them properly, and then sold or rented them to those who organized games. Imperial gladiatorial schools (*ludi imperiali*) appeared under the empire. They existed alongside private schools and were managed by procurators.

Gladiatorial schools must have sprung up soon after the emergence of gladiatorial games. However, the first reference to a gladiatorial school appears only at the end of the 2nd century BC: in 105 BC consul Publius Rutilius Rufus used *doctores* from Gaius Aurelius Scaurus' school to train his soldiers in the art of fencing. This school was probably in Capua.[242] Capua housed yet another school, that of Lentulus Batiatus, which became famous through Spartacus' revolt.[243] Caesar also owned a gladiatorial school in Capua, although he preferred to send gladiators to be trained in the houses of Roman equestrians, or even senators, who skilfully wielded a weapon. In his letters he insisted that the training of every gladiator be supervised and he often conducted lessons personally.[244] He later built another gladiatorial school, in Ravenna. Gladiators from his schools were famous for their training all over the empire and were called *Juliani*.[245]

The existence of gladiatorial schools in Rome can be traced at least as far back as the mid-1st century BC, when the conspirators against Caesar intended to resort to the services of the gladiators from a nearby school.[246] By the end of the 1st century AD, Rome already had four imperial schools. The most significant was the Great School (Ludus Magnus) situated near the Flavian Amphitheatre. All types of gladiators were trained here. An underground passage connected the school with the Colosseum, thus gladiators could appear in the arena unnoticed by the people.

Other schools had a more specific orientation: the Morning School (Ludus Matutinus) was designed to train prospective *venatores* and *bestiarii* (hence its name, as *venatio* was part of the morning programme); the Gallic School (Ludus Gallicus) trained *myrmillones*, while the Dacian School (Ludus Dacicus) admitted prisoners of war earmarked for the arena after Domitian's war with the Dacians.[247]

Gladiatorial school in Pompeii. The building was originally designed as a place where spectators could go out for a walk during the breaks between performances in the theatre, but it was later turned into a gladiatorial school. (Topfoto)

Only one school building, the Ludus Magnus, survives and its ruins can be seen near the Colosseum. Built of brick, it had probably three stories. Inside there was a courtyard with a portico and four fountains situated in the corners. The court looked like a small amphitheatre; the nine steps of its stands could house about 1,200 spectators, and in the centre of the northern and southern sides there were grandstands for very important guests. Two entrances situated on the main axis of the amphitheatre led to the arena. The central part of the eastern side was occupied by a large colonnaded room, which is believed to have been the sanctuary of the cult of the emperor. Gladiators inhabited the tiny crowded cells on the other sides. Supposedly, they could accommodate up to 1,000 men.

Apart from Rome, Capua and Ravenna, other Italian cities, namely Pompeii, Nola, Este and Praeneste, are also known to have had *ludi*. Many gladiatorial schools existed outside Italy, for example, in Britannia (modern Britain), Galatia, Cappadocia, Lycia, Pamphylia, Cilicia, Cyprus, Pontus, Paphlagonia, Gallia, Hispania (modern Spain), Germania and Raetia, and also in Alexandria in Aegyptus (modern Egypt). What is known as a gladiatorial school (or barracks) in Pompeii was not actually a classical instance of such an institution. This building, situated near the Great Theatre and having colonnaded porticoes on four sides, was designed for spectators to walk about during the intervals in the performances in the theatre. (A passage connected the two buildings.) It is, in fact, the oldest building of this kind in Italy – it dates as far back as the 1st century BC. In AD 62, after an earthquake had destroyed the gladiatorial school in Pompeii, this building was itself converted into a gladiatorial school. The passage connecting it with the theatre was blocked up and two-storey houses were built round the court, behind the colonnade. The ground floor was allotted for gladiators' cells, while on the first floor there were apartments for *lanistae*. A refectory and a kitchen were also present. The courtyard became the gladiators' training field. Numerous pieces of gladiatorial armament were found here during excavations, as well as 18 corpses of adults and one skeleton of a baby in a basket – the consequences of the tragic eruption of Vesuvius in 79.

Trainees within a particular gladiatorial school formed a *familia gladiatoria*, usually called by the name of its proprietor. Modest-scale shows often featured members of the same school, so contestants were members of one 'family'. It was only in games organized on a grand scale that several *ludi* took part.

Preparation of gladiators involved intensive training, a well-balanced diet, massage and regular medical examinations. Gladiators were generally fed on barley, which was considered extremely conducive to bodily health, hence the nickname of gladiators – *hordearii*, that is 'barley-eaters'.[248] Trainees were coached by *doctores*, generally ex-gladiators themselves. Usually each of these trainers was an expert in coaching only one particular type of gladiator, for example *retiarii* or *secutores*. There were professionals instructing in two or three disciplines, though.

Gladiators practised in a small-sized arena, usually situated in the centre of the gladiatorial school. The weapon used in training was blunt and as a rule, at least in earlier times, made of wood. The training shield (possibly a wicker one) and the wooden sword weighed twice as much as real fighting ones. Novices would practice with a wooden post dummy (*palus*)[249] – a similar training method was also used in the Roman Army. Only after this stage would they pass on to combat training with one another. Coaching included not only technical aspects of fencing, but psychological training as well. For example, many gladiators from Caligula's school were pronounced poor fighters because they could not watch an attacking sword without the reflex act of blinking.[250]

The *palus* also gave names to four ranks of gladiators: *primus palus*, *secundus palus*, *tertius palus* and *quartus palus*. A gladiator's reputation, however, and consequently his market price, was in the first place determined by his victories in real combats. Therefore, detailed archives kept record of each gladiator's victories and defeats and, most important, how often he had won the highest prize – the laurel wreath. The data were indicated in the games' programmes as well as on gladiators' tombstones. Moreover, after his first fight each gladiator was given a small tablet (*tessera gladiatoria*), which featured his name and the name of his owner; later the tablet carried a record of his number of combats and his victories.[251]

EVERYDAY LIFE AND THE SOCIAL STATUS OF GLADIATORS

Gladiators were chosen out of prisoners of war, slaves, condemned criminals and volunteers. Great wars brought considerable reinforcements to gladiatorial schools. During the Republican period, a prisoner of war used to fight with his traditional weapon or a similar one, hence the names given to some types of gladiator: *samnis*, *gallus*, *thraex*.

Gladiator slaves were the most numerous group. A master could sell a slave to a *lanista* (until Hadrian's rule even without offering any explanation or reason[252]) or a slave could be condemned to become a professional gladiator as a punishment.

In the Imperial period, death in the arena was just an ordinary form of execution. Criminals could be sentenced to it for committing murder, or robbery, arson, defilement of a temple, for high treason or military insurrection. Christians refusing to render homage to the emperor as a divine being often found themselves among those condemned to this kind of death. Sentences varied depending on the offence and the general feeling of the spectators. Some met their doom from a sword (*damnatus ad gladium*), others from wild animals (*damnatus ad bestias*) – the former were killed by professional gladiators. In any case, these wretches had no chance of remaining alive – unarmed and lacking special training all they could do was die. There was, however, a third possibility – to be sent to a gladiatorial school (*damnatus ad ludum*). A convict would long for this sentence, as at least he was given a chance to survive – after two years of training in a gladiatorial school he was to fight in the arena for three years. If by the end of this term he was still alive, he was awarded a wooden sword *rudis* as the sign of liberation.[253]

The last group comprised freeborn gladiator volunteers, who received the name of *auctorati*. They appeared in the Late Republican period and sharply increased in number during the empire. These voluntary fighters were particularly popular. An inscription on one of the graves in Pompeii says that free gladiators would meet in combat on the first day of the games and the next day gladiator slaves would fight.[254] *Auctorati* were appreciated for their high morale and reliable performance. An inscription discovered on the island of Thasos in the Aegean Sea informs us that for every ten gladiator slaves there were two *auctorati*, while another one, found in Asia Minor (from Aegae, Nemrut Kalesi), reads that the number of voluntary gladiators sometimes even exceeded that of gladiator slaves – three of the latter for each five of the former.[255]

Any freeborn person or a libertine coming to a gladiatorial school vowed in front of an official that he could be 'burned, bound, beaten, and killed with iron.'[256] Thus he acknowledged his employer's right to have a free hand in the question of his life or death during the entire term of the agreement. In return, he was paid 2,000 sesterces for a performance, stipulated by the law. After the expiry of the term, he could apply for another term. In this case his salary increased to 12,000 sesterces for a performance.[257] A voluntary gladiator could break a contract whenever he wished after paying the redemption fee.

Freeborn people became gladiators mostly for the sake of fame or money. We can hear obvious disapproval of such a choice in Tertullianus' words, written *c.* 200: 'What a great number of idlers have been induced by vainglory to undertake the trade of a gladiator, and some are vainglorious enough to take part in beast chasing, and believe that scars left by claws and teeth make them look more attractive.'[258] However, romantic stories based on a volunteer pursuing a noble aim are also known. Thus a young man from the city of Amastris took a job as a gladiator for a clearly agreed sum of 10,000 drachmae, which he needed to rescue a friend.[259] A young nobleman once became a gladiator to be able to pay for his father's funeral.[260]

The arena also saw many noble Romans participate, including senators and equestrians. They could be forced into combat by the whim of a particularly cruel emperor, but they often did it of their own accord. Studying gladiatorial art seems to have been in fashion among noble Romans, so many of them made it their hobby (almost as much as people nowadays are keen on mastering eastern martial arts or historical European swordsmanship). There were even regular youth teams (*juventus*) whose members studied gladiatorial art with the help of *doctores*.[261] These young people sometimes appeared in the arena (possibly fighting with wooden weapons), but on the whole they did not make professional gladiators or earn money in this way. Some emperors were fond of fighting with gladiators, too, as we have seen in the case of Commodus. Fighting in a single battle in private in his own house, he would kill an adversary without a moment's thought or cut off his hair, nose or ears. Nevertheless, when performing in public, he did not use a metal weapon and avoided shedding blood. He had a statue erected to himself and ordered an inscription to be made pointing out that he had defeated over 12,000 adversaries. Commodus was paid a million sesterces for every day spent in the arena.[262]

Known for his cruelty, Caligula fought with *myrmillones* with a wooden weapon, but afterwards killed his opponents, who deliberately yielded to the emperor, using a real metal weapon.[263] Titus, Hadrian, Lucius Verus, Didius Julianus (r. 193), Caracalla and Geta (r. 211–12) were more modest: they simply studied gladiatorial art.[264] There is a hypothesis that before he became emperor, Macrinus (r. 217–218) was a gladiator slave granted freedom.[265]

Auctorati were appreciated by many, however, some despised them as 'men who sell their blood.'[266] They were often placed on the same footing as pimps or actors[267] and in some towns (for instance, in Sarsina) it was even forbidden to bury them in a cemetery, like souteneurs or suicides who had hung themselves.[268] Perhaps only *lanistae*, considered as bad as pimps, were despised more.

As far back as 38 BC, a law was passed forbidding senators and, later, equestrians to fight as gladiators. The law, however, was disobeyed – after only ten years of the law a senator appeared in the arena and in AD 11 the ban on equestrians was lifted.

So at the time of Tiberius many 'profligate youths from higher classes' became gladiators of their own free will.[269] In 69 another act strictly forbidding equestrians to take part in gladiatorial combat was passed. According to Tacitus: 'under former *principes* they were inclined to do it with the help of money, but more often were forced to do it; *municipia* and colonies, vying with one another, sought to render the most corrupt young men gladiators by means of bribery.'[270]

The 1st and 2nd centuries even saw women gladiators in the arena. The first mention of *gladiatrici* refers to Nero's rule, when 'many ladies of distinction … disgraced themselves by appearing in the arena.'[271] It was also then that in order to celebrate the arrival of the Parthian King Tiridates III an extravagant show was organized, with both men and women of different ages fighting in the arena; moreover, all of them were Africans.[272] Another mention of *gladiatrici* is dated later, under Domitian.[273] Juvenalis (*c.* 60–140) vividly describes them engaged in combat:

> Why need I tell of the purple wraps and the wrestling-oils used by women? Who has not seen one of them smiting a stump, piercing it through and through with a foil, lunging at it with a shield, and going through all the proper motions? — a matron truly qualified to blow a trumpet at the Floralia! Unless, indeed, she is nursing some further ambition in her bosom, and is practising for the real arena... What a fine thing for a husband, at an auction of his wife's effects, to see her belt and armlets and plumes put up for sale, with a gaiter that covers half the left leg; or if she fight another sort of battle, how charmed you will be to see your young wife disposing of her greaves!... See how she pants as site goes through her prescribed exercises; how she bends under the weight of her helmet; how big and coarse are the bandages which enclose her haunches; and then laugh when she lays down her arms and shows herself to be a woman![274]

Women gladiators, however, seem to have been a comparatively rare sight in the amphitheatres; neither were gladiatorial games organized by a woman a common event.[275] In 200, after particularly numerous duels between women gladiators, Emperor Septimius Severus forbade women to perform in the arena once and for all.[276]

While slave gladiators were only called by name, freeborn gladiators had their family names indicated too (for instance, Ti. Claudius Firmus, T. Flavius Incitatus, M. Ulpius Felix, P. Aelius Aplus). Meanwhile, many gladiators, slaves as well as freeborn, preferred to be called by nicknames chosen from amongst the names of either distinguished representatives of fauna (Lion, Tiger, Dove), mythological characters (Achilles, Hercules, Hermes), or famous gladiators dearly loved by the public (Columbus, Triumphus). Some inscriptions carry the elaboration 'lib' following the gladiator's name; it is unclear, though, whether it stands for *liber* – freeborn citizen, or *libertus* – freed gladiator. When, however, we see the word *rudiarius* in an epigram, it obviously refers to a gladiator who had received his freedom together with the wooden *rudis* sword.

What were a gladiator's chances of surviving? What was the average span of a gladiator's life? We know that even a defeated gladiator often quitted the arena alive. But how often could a fighter who was knocked out count on mercy (*missio*)? The attitude to defeated gladiators was varied in different epochs. Very little detailed information is available about the Republican period. One gets the impression,

Oppostite:
The tombstone of the gladiator Aquilo, who had been a slave but had gained freedom fighting in the arena. Judging by the relief Aquilo was either a *myrmillo* or a *thraex*. Early 1st century AD. (Römisch-Germanisches Museum, Köln. Author's collection)

Part of the Roman Colosseum, showing the tall Roman pillars in front, AD 80. (Hubertus Kanus / Topfoto)

however, that a combat frequently ended in the death of a gladiator. An important factor was the political mission of the *munera*. Games were usually organized to win over public sympathies in the struggle for power. The more pompous and bloody the show, the longer it was remembered. Besides, the *editor* was led by the public, as a rule: 'they hold shows of their own, and win applause by slaying whomsoever the mob with a turn of the thumb bids them slay.'[277]

In the Imperial period, the political role of gladiatorial games changed, but the decision taken by an *editor* still depended on the public. Augustus introduced laws regulating *munera* rules and forbade *sine missione* combats — encounters in which the death of a gladiator was stipulated at the start.[278] Ville has analysed the surviving data of about 100 single combats which took place in the 1st century. The results of his calculations are revealing. Out of 200 participating gladiators, only 19 died. Moreover, the real number of combatants who were refused a *missio* is even less, as at least one of these 19 must have received a mortal blow in action and somebody else might have died from wounds afterwards. Thus, the chances of a gladiator surviving the arena at this time were about 9:1, and for a defeated combatant, 4:1.[279]

Deaths in the arena grew sharply in the 2nd and especially the 3rd centuries. According to Ville, every second single combat ended in the death of a gladiator. Hence, a gladiator's chances of survival in combat fell to 3:1, and the loser had equal chances of life or death. These figures mean that granting life to a defeated gladiator was quite common in the Early Imperial period and only a combatant whose fighting abilities were obviously much below average could be punished by death. Later, however, the situation changed dramatically. In the 2nd and 3rd centuries, the killing of a loser became the norm, and only an extraordinarily gifted fighter was granted *missio*.

It is possible that the 2nd and 3rd centuries saw the return of *sine missione* combats to popularity, with the death of one of the participants predestined. Otherwise it is difficult to explain the following inscription on the pedestal of the statue of Publius Bebius Justus, erected in 249: 'He, in Miturns, during four days, brought out 11 pairs of gladiators, and out of them 11 gladiators of first class from Campania were killed, as well as ten bloodthirsty bears.'[280] So each defeated gladiator was killed. All of them were first-class combatants, moreover; they came from Campania, a region at all times famed for the training it offered to gladiators. It is incredible that not one of those famous combatants displayed his masterly skill.

The above statistics are useful in calculating the length of a gladiator's life. It was not often that professional gladiators fought in the arena. Big gladiatorial games were comparatively rare, so a gladiator would be idle for months. If we assume that he performed in the arena three times a year on average, even in the 1st century his career should have lasted no more than four years before it was ended by death. This is an average index, though. In real life, a dull or poorly trained novice would usually meet his death in one of the first encounters, while gifted professionals, multiple winners, lived much longer. This imbalance had several causes. First, the weakest fighters fell away in the first fights and only the strongest remained. Second, no training can match the reality of combat, therefore a veteran was endowed with a far better experience and felt more confident. And last, but not least, a veteran's fans would not allow a famous combatant to die even when he was defeated. A veteran gladiator could have much more hope for a *missio* than an unknown fighter. This fact accounts for the existence of champions who survived 60, 80, 88, 107, 125 and even 150 combats.[281] These figures show that veteran gladiators were engaged more often than novices, and probably went on tours to other cities besides.

Judging from tombstones, the average lifespan of a gladiator was about 27 years, which is close to the average lifespan of most Romans. However, tombstones must have only been put on the graves of famous combatants. Numerous slave gladiators killed at the beginning of their careers would hardly be honoured with such memorials. So it can be assumed that for the most part gladiators died at the age of 18–25, on average. But there is no rule without an exception. The Syrian gladiator Flamma remained alive for 30 years, although he tempted fate permanently – four times he was awarded with a *rudis*, and every time returned to the arena. In total, he gained 25 victories, received four *missio* and had nine draws (*stans missus*). He began his career at the age of 17, which means that he appeared in the arena every fourth month on average.[282]

Gladiators' attitude to their trade varied. The fairly common conception of gladiators driven out to die in the arena with sticks or hot irons seems somewhat one-sided and not necessarily true. Certainly, several cases are known of gladiators committing suicide rather than face the arena – the suicide of 29 Saxon prisoners of war due for gladiatorial games in 393 was mentioned above. Seneca offers a few more examples. During a *naumachia*, one of the participants deliberately pierced his throat with a javelin; another one being driven to a morning performance feigned sleepiness and bent his head down so low that it was caught between the spokes of a wheel and his neck was broken. A German suffocated himself by pushing a stick with a sponge used for cleaning toilets down into his throat; evidently he was unwilling to face the beasts at a morning show.[283] It seems, however, that most of

those who committed suicide were not professional gladiators but convicts sentenced to death. This conclusion is supported by their participation in either *naumachia* or a morning performance with animals. Alongside these facts there are also mentions of gladiators who complained about not being invited into the arena as often as they wished.[284]

Many high-ranking Romans acquired gladiatorial troupes not only for entertainment (for instance, at a banquet) but as bodyguards[285] or hired murderers.[286] It is curious that, unlike a *lanista*, a noble Roman citizen could rent out or sell his troupe of gladiators without being held in contempt. It was considered a *lanistae*'s trade and principal job, while for noble Romans it was looked upon just as a sideline income.

Troupes of gladiators were fairly often used in skirmishes between rival political groups; this was a particular characteristic of the 1st century BC. In 59 BC, Scaurus accused his opponents in the struggle for the consulate of having an armed detachment consisting of 300 men at their disposal. Marcus Antonius' (also known as Mark Antony) personal guard was 6,000 men strong.[287] Unfortunately, no exact data about the profession or social position of these people is available, but gladiators were undoubtedly to be found among them. What is known for sure is that *crupellarii* were very active during the Gaul insurrection in AD 21.[288] Armed gladiatorial detachments played so notable a part in the Catilinarian Conspiracy (a rebellion led by Lucius Sergius Catilina) that in 63 BC the Senate passed a special resolution which decreed that most gladiators should be withdrawn from Rome to other cities.[289] In 49 BC, early in the Roman civil war, Pompey, fearing Caesar's gladiators, distributed other gladiators amongst Roman families as bodyguards.[290] Opposing Antony, Decimus Brutus had 'a great number of gladiators' in his troops.[291]

Many emperors reinforced their armies with gladiators. Otho (r. 69) enlisted 2,000 gladiators in his forces. It was a 'shameful sort of auxiliary troops, which, however, at the time of civil wars, was not looked down upon even by honest commanders' – this sharp comment was made about gladiatorial troops by Tacitus.[292] Indeed, trained for fighting in single combat but not in a battle formations, gladiators did little to help Otho, as well as Vitellius, whom they deserted for his more successful opponent Vespasian, who also received scant benefit from the service.[293] In the course of the assault on Tarracina, only 'a few gladiators offered resistance to the enemy and sell their lives at good price; the others rushed for the ships, but death awaited them there too.'[294] Averse to gladiatorial games in general, Marcus Aurelius created a special gladiatorial unit under a significant name – 'The Obedient'[295] – to be used in the war against the Marcomanni. In the course of the civil war in AD 193, Didius Julianus reinforced his army with Capuan gladiators.[296]

Like any other property, gladiatorial troops could be sold or bought. Caligula organized special auctions to sell off gladiators who had survived his entertaining shows at fantastical prices. According to Suetonius:

> he exposed to sale by auction, the remains of the apparatus used in the public spectacles; and exacted such biddings, and raised the prices so high, that some of the purchasers were ruined, and bled themselves to death. There is a well-known story told of Aponius Saturninus, who happening to fall asleep as he sat on a bench at the sale, Caius called out to the auctioneer, not to overlook the praetorian personage who nodded to him so often; and accordingly the salesman went on, pretending to take the nods for tokens of assent, until thirteen gladiators were knocked down to him at the sum of nine millions of sesterces, he being in total ignorance of what was doing.[297]

A gladiator who was granted freedom (a *rudiarius*) could take the job again, now as *auctoratus*, or as a *doctor* in a gladiatorial school or a judge (*summa rudis* or *secunda rudis*).

A famous gladiator had crowds of worshippers. Inscriptions preserved in the gladiatorial school in Pompeii lead us to believe that the followers did not even

Oppostite:
Tombstone of the gladiator Nikephoros. Here he is armed as a *provocator* – wearing a breastplate *cardiophylax*, *manica* on the right arm and probably holding a helmet and shield under his left arm.
(Archaeological Museum, Hierapolis. Author's collection)

153

miss training sessions.[298] There were also admirers of certain categories of gladiators: those following gladiators who used a big *scutum* shield (*myrmillones*) were called *scutarii*, while those who preferred gladiators using a small *parmula* shield (*thracians*) were called *parmularii*. The 2nd and 3rd centuries saw particularly ferocious quarrels between *scutarii* and *parmularii*.[299] On the whole, however, fans were quieter in the amphitheatre than teams of Blues, Greens, Reds and Whites fans at chariot races in the Circus.

Many emperors also admired gladiators of a certain type. Commodus adored *secutores*, Caligula worshipped *thracians*, while Domitian preferred *myrmillones*. Emperors also had favourites among gladiators. Thus, Caligula made a *thraex* head of his bodyguard detachment consisting of Germans,[300] while Nero presented the *myrmillo* Spicillus with the property and palaces of senators fallen into disgrace.[301]

Naturally, gladiators did not leave women indifferent to their powerful muscles and fighting prowess in the arena. Women were not so much interested in the nuances of combat as they were attracted by the appearance of their lovers and the halo of fame that surrounded them. From numerous inscriptions on the walls of Pompeii, we can learn about local lady-killers: a *thraex* called Celadus, for example was labelled as the 'girls' joy and dream', and a *retiarius* Crescentus, was known as the 'girls' sovereign and healer'.[302]

Many noble Roman women and even some empresses could not resist a gladiator's charm. It is supposed that Curtius Rufus (of the same name as the famous historian), who achieved the post of consul and was awarded triumphal honours and the province of Africa, as well as Emperor Commodus, were sons of gladiators.[303] Juvenalis denounces the wife of a senator for running away with a former gladiator Sergius, who was disfigured by scars and swellings but was a gladiator, so was worthy of committing the sin:

And what were the youthful charms which captivated Eppia? What did she see in him to allow herself to be called 'a she-Gladiator'? Her dear Sergius had already begun to shave; a wounded arm gave promise of a discharge, and there were sundry deformities in his face: a scar caused by the helmet, a huge wen upon his nose, a nasty humour always trickling from his eye. But then he was a gladiator! It is this that transforms these fellows into Hyacinthuses! It was this that she preferred to children and to country, to sister and to husband. What these women love is the sword: had this same Sergius received his discharge, he would have been no better than a Veiento.[304]

Eight bodies of men and one female body were found in one of the rooms of the gladiatorial school in Pompeii. Expensive jewellery lay by the side of the woman – she was a rich woman. We shall never know what she was doing in the gladiatorial school, but perhaps one of the gladiators was her lover.

Many gladiators were married or had mistresses – numerous tombstones laid on one gladiator's grave by his wife testify to that fact. Some of these women shared the burdens of life in the gladiatorial barracks, but they were looked upon with scorn, which is clear from the very name *ludia* – the word is partly abusive and means, besides the wife of a gladiator, a dancer and actress (both professions with poor reputations). We also know about graves built by gladiators for their wives, which also shows the gladiators' comparative economic independence – the fact that they were able to bury them in graves and have gravestones means that they had their own money. There are tombstones erected by friends from a *familia gladiatoria*. Epitaphs on the tombs of gladiators are in the same fashion as those on soldiers' gravestones: the name is followed by the type of weapon he fought with, his native country, the number of combats he had fought and the years of his life.[305]

CHAPTER VII

THE DAY OF
THE SHOW

It remains for us to explore the typical daily programme of a gladiatorial show, focusing on the order of events in a show from the time of Augustus (r. 27 BC–AD 14. The morning programme was comprised of a *venatio*, including executions of criminals sentenced to be killed by beasts. The main executions of criminals, competitions of athletes and performances given by comic actors usually took place at midday, during a break after the *venatio*. Gladiatorial combats, the culmination of the programme, began in the afternoon.

The day's performance began with a *pompa*. Accompanied by lictors and musicians, the organizer of the games was the first to appear in the arena. He was followed by carriers of tablets, which informed the spectators of the punishments to which the criminals were sentenced and what pairs of gladiators would take part in the games. Then the heroes of the day entered the arena – gladiators, *venatores* and the condemned convicts.

A representation of a *pompa* can be seen in the upper part of one of the reliefs from Pompeii. Two lictors wearing *togae* and carrying *fasces* are marching at the head of the procession. *Fasces* were a bundle of rods tied with a band, and they served as emblems of official power. When carried outside the walls of Rome, each bundle also contained an axe. The lictors are followed by three trumpeters, followed in their turn by four men carrying a *ferculum*, a transportable platform for carrying statues, on their shoulders. Outside the amphitheatre these statues were usually those of Hercules, Mars, Nemesis and Nike. In this case, however, the *ferculum* supports two states of bent armourers, probably making armour for gladiators. Behind the *ferculum*, the artist shows two figures carrying tablets with information for the public and a palm branch for the victor. The next figure is a Roman nobleman in holiday attire, undoubtedly the *editor* himself. He has half turned his head to his six assistants carrying gladiators' helmets and shields. This group is sometimes taken for a representation of *probatio armorum* – the checking of the armour before combat. Gladiators' armament was indeed examined before combat in order to eliminate dirty tricks and to demonstrate that all the combatants had equal chances. This examination, however, was only applied to weapons proper – swords, daggers, spears – while the people in the relief are holding nothing but helmets and shields, which did not require any inspection. Hence this part of the relief would be more correctly interpreted as part of a ceremonial procession. Helmets and shields were carried separately from the gladiators to give the public a chance to see the bare faces and muscles of the warriors.

Further along the relief there is a man holding an unidentifiable object, followed by one more trumpeter with a signal horn. The procession closes with two men

A fragment of the famous mosaic from Zliten (Libya) showing various scenes from gladiatorial games. At the top (from left to right) there is a bust of an *editor*, musicians, a stretcher to take away the dead or wounded, and an umpire holding one of the *equites* by the hand, expecting a verdict. The bottom row comprises combat between a *retiarius* and a *secutor*, a *thraex–myrmillo* pair and a *hoplomachus–myrmillo* pair (the *myrmillo* is holding up his finger and the umpire is stopping the fight). The gladiator on the extreme right is a *provocator*, his opponent (also a *provocator*) cannot be seen in this photograph. AD 200. (German Archaeological Institute)

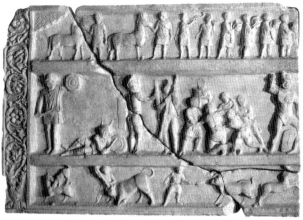

A relief from Pompeii showing *munus* and *venatio*. The upper row is taken up by a ceremonial procession (*pompa*). Gladiatorial fights are represented in the middle – from left to right there are two equites; a group consisting of two gladiators, umpires and assistants; two *provocatores*; two groups each consisting of three men (perhaps, *paegniarii* and their assistants); a *hoplomachus* and a *myrmillo* (on the extreme right). *Venatores* fighting with animals, as well as three *bestiarii* at the moment of letting beasts out onto the arena, can be seen in the bottom row. AD 20–50. (Museo Archeologico Nazionale, Napoli)

leading horses, probably for *equites*. Gladiators themselves are not shown here, although they were an integral part of the *pompa* and the most exciting view for the spectators.

A *venatio* usually opened with more or less inoffensive shows like a demonstration of exotic species of fauna or performing animals. This display was followed by a beast hunt, animal fights and *taurocatapsia*. The latter seems to be a rare item of the games. A *venatio* culminated in a fight between *venatores* and beasts. Tearing criminals to pieces by wild animals was displayed during a dinner break or just before it.

Gladiatorial combats opened with a prelude (*prolusio*), with pairs of gladiators (*lusorii*) fighting with non-lethal weapons. The 'toy' weapon (*arma lusoria*) was probably an ordinary wooden type used in training. The prelude prepared the public for more exciting spectacles and gave gladiators a chance to warm up their muscles. *Prolusio* was followed by *probatio armorum* – testing deadly weapons (*ferrum acutum*) – checking the firmness, sharpness, and other characteristics of a weapon.

Only then did proper gladiatorial combat begin. The fights were always opened by *equites*, if they were on the programme. The order of appearance of the other types of gladiator was not so strictly fixed and could vary from game to game.

Gladiators were usually engaged in pairs. Less often, a *retiarius* and two *secutores* fought to occupy the *pons*. Occasionally, at a very big *munus*, a battle between teams of gladiators was arranged. These team battles were called *gregatim* (lit. 'in a crowd'). As in *naumachia*, the battle was more often than not based upon a mythological or historical subject. It is unlikely that first-class and consequently expensive gladiators would have taken part in this mass butchery. Most probably second-rate gladiators were used or even criminals sentenced to capital punishment.

With the appearance of a gladiator in the arena, his name and service record were announced by a public crier. Not all the spectators, particularly those sitting in the upper rows, could hear the voice of the crier, so a large tablet containing information about his name and recorded victories was probably carried in front of a gladiator.

It seems that before starting combat, gladiators were allowed to display their abilities and skills in a certain kind of art. For instance, a fresco from the amphitheatre in Pompeii (only preserved as a copy today) shows a *hoplomachus* and a *myrmillo* standing opposite each other; an umpire (*summa rudis*), recognizable by his long stick, stands between them. Both gladiators are almost completely equipped; only helmets and weapons are held at the ready by their assistants. The *hoplomachus* is playing a curved trumpet, evidently taking the opportunity to win public sympathies as well as to vex his opponent.

Fighting usually continued unbroken until one party gained a victory – there were no rounds. True, on exceptional occasions – such as a combat lasting too long and both gladiators being exhausted – the umpire could announce a break (*diludium*), during which the combatants might be given first aid or just massaged.

Two judges – an umpire (*summa rudis*) and his assistant (*secunda rudis*) – watched the fighting. Their primary task was to make sure that the rules of combat (*dictata*) were obeyed, for a gladiatorial combat was not a primitive exchange of blows. Sadly, little if anything at all is known about those rules. On exceptional occasions, when the combatants were not zealous enough or disobeyed the rules, the umpire struck them with his stick – an indispensable attribute of an umpire. When this was to no avail, the assistant could resort to a whip, a torch or even a red-hot iron. These measures were only applied to convicts condemned to death though, not to professional gladiators.

A combat was considered over when one of the following three conditions was fulfilled. First, one of the gladiators was dead or mortally wounded, or his wounds were so serious that he was unable to fight. Second, weakened by injuries or extreme exhaustion one of the combatants surrendered. Then he dropped or lowered his shield or trident (if he was a *retiarius*) and held up his arm with a finger (usually forefinger of his left hand) stretched out.[306] Seeing this conventional sign, the umpire stood up between the combatants and saw to it that the winner did no harm to the defeated. Should the victorious gladiator have failed to halt immediately and displayed continuing zeal, the umpire intercepted his hand with a weapon and held the limb fast, preventing him from any further offensive actions. Voluntary

Bronze figurine of a *thraex*. The gladiator has put his shield on the ground and raised the forefinger of his left hand to show he is submitting. 1st–2nd centuries AD. (British Museum, London. Author's collection)

A mosaic discovered in Appian Way, Rome, depicting two stages of a combat between the *equites Habilis* and *Maternus*. Two umpires are watching the combat. 4th century AD. (Photo Archive, National Archaeology Museum, Madrid)

surrender of one of the competitors seems to have been a common outcome of a fight. There was also a third condition: if both gladiators had been fighting for a long time, demonstrating their valour and extraordinary potential while unable to win a decisive victory, the spectators could show with applause that they wished both gladiators to be pardoned. Then the combat ended with a draw and both gladiators would leave the arena on foot (*stans missus*).

When a combat ended with the surrender of one of the fighters, his fate depended on the *editor*'s decision, but as a rule, the *editor* allowed for the spectators' opinion. Having shown courage, good fighting spirit and skill, a gladiator could count upon the public sympathy and, consequently, on being granted his life. When most of the spectators shouted 'missum!' or 'mitte!' the *editor* gave a sign to the umpire to let the defeated gladiator go. Should, however, the surrendering combatant have demonstrated inadequate or ineffective fighting, he would hardly have gained sympathy. A dissatisfied or just bloodthirsty public would declaim 'jugula, verbera, ure!' ('cut, beat, burn').

Opinions still differ as to the gesture that went along with the shouts. In the 19th century, it was generally believed that a verdict for death was accompanied by a thumb-down sign while a call for mercy was indicated by the thumb-up sign. The author of this belief is unknown, but no evidence (written or iconographic) exists in favour of this opinion. Only Juvenalis mentions in one of his satires that gladiators were sentenced to death by the turn of a thumb ('and win applause by

19th century drawings from a fresco which once adorned the podium wall of the amphitheatre in Pompeii. At the top, a *hoplomachus* and a *myrmillo* are ready to begin combat. An umpire (*summa rudis*), easily recognisable by his long stick, is standing between them. Nearby their assistants hold their helmets and weapons. Before the combat the *hoplomachus* is demonstrating his skill in playing a curved trumpet. (Museo Archeologico Nazionale, Napoli)

The finale of a combat between *equites* gladiators. To the sounds of trumpets someone (most likely to be the organiser of the games) gives a signal with his hand: the thumb is pressed in, the forefinger and the middle finger are stretched out. This gesture is thought to mean mercy (*missio*). Late 1st century BC. (Staatliche Antikensammlungen und Glyptothek, München)

slaying whomsoever the mob with a turn of the thumb wishes'[307]). He does not indicate, however, what way the thumb must be turned. Horatius' words are even less clear: he speaks of an encouraging gesture made with thumbs (possibly of both hands), but he speaks about a children's game and not about gladiatorial contests.[308]

Today, the 19th-century interpretation is considered doubtful. Thus, Junkelmann believes that a death verdict was opined with the thumb-up sign; he does not say anything about a fist with a thumb-down at all.[309] In another work he suggests that no extended-thumb hand action was of decisive significance.[310] Other historians see things differently. One of them states that a demand to deal a mortal blow to a defeated gladiator was confirmed by a thumb turned chestways,[311] while another says that it must have been an open palm;[312] according to a third version, a thumb-down sign meant mercy,[313] and a fourth suggests that mercy was granted with the wave of a handkerchief.[314]

It should be noted that none of the researchers offers any convincing evidence, so each version can only be considered as supposition and the question remains undoubtedly open. What is quite clear, though, is that the traditional view should be regarded with a large pinch of salt, as it is unconfirmed by sources. The only relief that is probably related to this dramatic moment shows a defeated gladiator sitting on the arena floor, while the victor is standing with a sword raised over him. Someone, supposedly the *editor*, is making a gesture with his hand, in which the thumb is clasped but the forefinger and middle finger are stretched out. Possibly, this gesture meant mercy. On the whole, the lack of attention to this fatal moment displayed by ancient sculptors and artists is indeed surprising. Only one in a huge number of gladiatorial images represents – and only supposedly – this stage of a combat. Could this gesture be of no significance at all?

Whatever the thumb-up or thumb-down signal meant, it remains a mystery how the *editor* could know the opinion of the majority of the spectators. We know that in the eyes of the organizer of games the opinion of the crowds occupying the top seats meant much more than that of senators or equestrians. But in big amphitheatres it was practically impossible to make out what sign people in the top rows were making. Shouts, too, inevitably merged into a blurry hum. We can assume that attendants made rounds of the rows with the express purpose of finding out the feelings of the public, and informed the *editor* of the prevailing opinion.

After a death sentence was confirmed by the *editor* (*pollice verso*), the defeated gladiator knelt in front of the victor clasping the *editor*'s knees in his arms – provided he had strength enough to do so – or rested his hands against the ground or put them behind his back. Even at that moment he did not take off his helmet and remained a faceless combat machine. As we have seen, however, some particularly bloodthirsty emperors enjoyed looking into the face of a dying man. Thus, Claudius ordered every losing *retiarius*, even one whose fall was accidental, to be dealt a mortal blow[315] (*retiarii* being the only gladiators who never wore helmets), and Commodus acted as a *secutor* in gladiatorial contests – it offered him a chance of killing an adversary with his own hands while looking him in the face.

The fatal blow was usually struck into the throat, or more rarely to the chest, of a gladiator. If the gladiator was unable to kneel, he would lie down on his belly and the winner thrust a sword into his back so that the sword penetrated to the heart. The moment when the loser was struck the final blow, when he 'received iron'

The finale of a combat between a *secutor* and a *retiarius*. The latter is holding the forefinger of his right hand up to show he is submitting. Submission is mostly demonstrated in images with a raised forefinger of the left hand. However *retiarii* and left-hander gladiators must have raised the forefinger of the right hand as the arm-guard *manica* on the left hand could prevent a gladiator from making his intention clear. AD 175. (Colchester Museum. Author's collection)

Part of the tombstone from a *retiarius'* grave discovered in Appian Way, Rome. It shows five *retiarius–secutor* pairs in combat. All *retiarii* are victorious. One of the *secutores* is holding his hand up asking for the interruption of the fight, the rest are already kneeling, ready to receive the fatal blow. Judging by the number of gladiators about to be killed, it is a *sine missione* combat. 3rd century AD. (Musei Capitolini, Rome)

(*ferum recipere*), the spectators cried 'Habet!' ('That's it / hit it / got it!'). The cries 'Habet! Hoc habet!' ('Hit it! Again hit it!') accompanied every successive strike during combat.

A gladiator was expected to face death with honour – any resistance or plea for mercy was received with extreme disgust. Meeting death with dignity was considered proof of bravery and courage, which every honourable Roman citizen should demonstrate. 'He died like a gladiator' was the highest praise for a soldier. It exemplified firmness at the last moment of his life, an even more vaunted quality than the prowess he displayed in combat. Many ancient authors extolled the gladiator's heroism in their works. Here we see Cicero praising the gladiators' bravery:

What wounds will the gladiators bear, who are either barbarians, or the very dregs of mankind? How do they, who are trained to it, prefer being wounded to basely avoiding it? How often do they prove that they consider nothing but giving satisfaction to their masters or to the people? For when covered with wounds, they send to their masters to learn their pleasure: if it is their will, they are ready to lie down and die. What gladiator, of even moderate reputation, ever gave a sigh? Who ever turned pale? Who ever disgraced himself either in the actual combat, or even when about to die? Who that had been defeated ever drew in his neck to avoid the stroke of death? So great is the force of practice, deliberation, and custom! Shall this, then, be done by a Samnite rascal, worthy of his trade; and shall a man born to glory have so soft a part in his soul as not to be able to fortify it by reason and reflection?[316]

A dead gladiator was taken away in a special cart through the Porta Libitinensis (Libitina was the goddess of death and burying) to a mortuary (*spoliarium*), where his throat was cut once more, just in case. Then he was undressed and prepared for burial. Many professional gladiators, particularly famous combatants, were buried according to Roman customs, to which numerous surviving tombstones still bear witness. Never were professional gladiators, even dead ones, pulled away from the

This mosaic, discovered in Appian Way, Rome, shows a *retiarius* Kalendio in combat with *secutor* Astyanax. The beginning of the combat, with the *secutor* caught in the *retiarius'* net, can be seen at the bottom. The *retiarius*, however, failed to make use of his success and the fighting took a different turn. In the top picture, the defeated *retiarius* has lost his trident and is only armed with a dagger. The umpire is announcing *secutor* Astyanax victorious. The inscription pronounces Kalendio dead (the letter Ø). Early 4th century AD. (Photo Archive, National Archaeology Museum, Madrid)

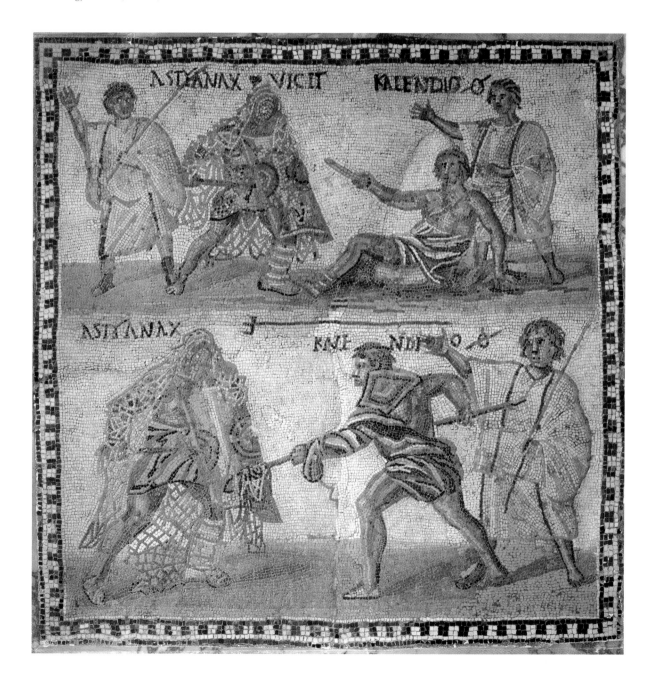

arena with hooks. Such handling was only applied to the bodies of condemned criminals (*noxii*).

The servants in the *spoliarium*, together with those who took dead gladiators away from the arena, wore costumes of the gods Charon (the ferryman who conveyed the souls of the dead in Greek mythology) and Mercury (who in Roman beliefs accompanied the dead to the underworld). However, these costumed attendants possibly only appeared in the arena at midday, during the execution of criminals. It is also possible that the testing of bodies with hot iron rods (to see if they were dead), as well as dealing a fatal blow with a hammer, was only applied to condemned criminals, not to professional gladiators.[317]

Quite a different lot was in store for a wounded gladiator who had been allowed to leave the arena alive. He was given the best possible medical treatment. A professional gladiator was so expensive that both the *lanista* and the *editor* were anxious to keep him alive and healthy. When a gladiator died or became disabled for a long time, the *editor* had to pay much more than the cost of his participation in a combat.

Gladiatorial duel pictured on a flask. In the foreground a victorious *myrmillo* is about to deal a fatal blow to the defeated *thraex*. The latter seems seriously wounded, unable to kneel, so the *myrmillo* is directing his weapon in the *thraex*' back. 2nd–3rd centuries AD. (Römisch-Germanisches Museum, Köln. Author's collection)

As the defeated gladiator was, one way or another, leaving the arena, the winner climbed up the stairs to the *editor's* seat to receive his award. This was usually a palm branch (*palma*) and a considerable sum of money (*praemium*). The premium was the gladiator's property whether he was a freeman or a slave, but the sum depended on the gladiator's status: a slave could not get a sum exceeding one-fifth of his market price and a voluntary gladiator's premium was no more than one-fourth.[318] A gladiator could also be awarded a laurel wreath or a crown, of which the latter was more common in the east of the empire. In the Republican and Early Imperial periods, a laurel wreath was considered the highest decoration, only given in exceptional cases, while in the Late Imperial period it was handed out as often as a palm branch. Gladiators were sometimes awarded with other symbols of honour, such as a necklace (*torques*) or an honorary *hasta* spear.

The wooden *rudis* sword was a special award given rarely and for numerous victories only. For the gladiator it meant that he was no longer obliged to fight in the arena. For the *editor* it was the costliest present, as he had to repay the *lanista* the full cost of this gladiator or let him have an equally strong combatant in exchange.

On receiving his awards, the gladiator made a lap of honour around the arena, waving his palm branch. The result of every encounter was registered in the gladiator's service record. Information concerning the outcome of combat can be seen in numerous reliefs, mosaics and graffiti. The letter 'V' (short for *viciit*) stood for a victor, 'M' (from *missus*) for a pardoned gladiator, 'P' (from *periit* – perished) or 'Q' (from *Qanatoz* – death) meant that the gladiator was either killed in combat or met with his death afterward. Such abbreviations as 'ST.M' (from *stans missus*) and 'M.P' (from *missus, periit*) are also found. The first meant that the combat ended with a draw and both combatants left the arena alive, the second stood for a pardoned gladiator who died from wounds later.

Music accompanied not only *pompa*, but also other events of the day of performance. Even gladiatorial combats in the amphitheatre were accompanied by a simple melody, which gave the action a rhythm. The main instruments of musicians in the amphitheatres were a curved *cornu* trumpet, a long and straight *tuba* trumpet and a short *lituus* horn. A signal to start fighting seems to have been given with a double oboe (*tibia impares*). In the 1st century, under Nero, a water organ (*hydraulus*) was added to these instruments and quickly gained popularity; its simple melodies became a common accompaniment of games in the amphitheatre.

CONCLUSION

CRAVING BLOOD OR BLOODY SPORT?

Romans are often accused of excessive bloodthirstiness because of their predilection for gladiatorial fights. A modern man finds it hard to imagine that pleasure could be derived from watching murderous violence, the blood and slaughter of man and beast. It is worth remembering, however, that the mentality of ancient and medieval people differed greatly from our own. Public torture and execution were common sights throughout the history of humanity until quite recently. Both ecclesiastical and temporal authorities considered them the norm of life, and even encouraged such practices. These actions were performed in large squares, as a rule, and attracted crowds of people from nobles to gutter-dwellers, who gathered to revel in the sufferings of the victims.

Incidentally, modern sports that to a certain degree involve violence (boxing, karate and others) today attract millions of fans to stadiums or TV sets. The death of a participant is evidently not intended in these sports, but its possibility cannot be ruled out either. Cases are known of fighters falling dead in the ring or dying from injuries in hospitals; as to injuries, they are quite a common spectacle. It is the physical risk that these and other martial arts contain that often attracts people to them in the first place.

Indeed, what about the huge crowds of spectators, locals and tourists, who go to see a *corrida* bullfight? In what way is a *corrida* different in principle from a *venatio*? Statistics tells us that 398 men were killed in *corrida* from 1747 to 1962, among them 51 professional matadors, 153 novice matadors, 132 banderilleros, 60 picadors and two clowns. The *corrida*, quite clearly, is also a bloody sport. Moreover, in some ways we are crueller than Romans with respect to animals: generally, a bull is killed in a *corrida* whatever the outcome of the encounter, while in a *venatio* a victorious beast was granted life.

Furthermore, consider our addiction to television programmes featuring accidents or violent incidents, and how many people enjoy bloody thrillers and detective stories? No doubt we feel horror and compassion watching real or fictional misfortunes, yet our magnetic attraction to misfortune is apparent – think of why crowds of people gather around a large-scale traffic accident. It is not surprising, therefore, that most Romans, whose evaluation of the value of human life differed from ours anyway, watched gladiatorial fighting with keen interest. For all its violence, it was a professional sport, like boxing or karate today. Compared to modern fighting in the ring, gladiatorial contests were much more colourfully furnished and bore an integral element of a theatrical performance. It was, however, far more dangerous, as human life itself was at stake.

APPENDICES

TYPES OF GLADIATOR, THEIR ARMAMENT, OPPONENTS AND THE TIME OF THEIR POPULARITY			
Type of Gladiator	Arms and Armour	Time of Their Popularity	Opponent
Andabata	'Blind' helmet without eyeholes.	Republican period	*Andabata*
Arbelas	Helmet, scale armour or mail (?), two greaves, sword and weapon with crescent-shaped blade and tubular vambrace.	1st century BC (?)–2nd–3rd centuries AD	*Retiarius or arbelas*
Dimachaerus	Close-fitting helmet with brims, short greaves on both legs, mail (?), two swords or daggers.	2nd–3rd centuries AD	*Dimachaerus* (?)
Eques	Broad-brimmed helmet without crest, *manica* arm-guard, round medium-size shield, spear (when mounted), sword (when on foot).	1st century BC–4th century AD	*Eques*
Essedarius	Helmet without brims, *manica* arm-guard on the right arm, oval shield, sword.	1st century AD–3rd century AD	*Essedarius*
Gallus	Probably helmet, greave, large shield (*scutum*) and sword.	(?)–mid-1st century BC	*Gallus* (?)
Hoplomachus	Helmet, *manica* arm-guard, high greaves, small round shield, spear, sword or dagger.	Late Republican–end of gladiatorial games	*Myrmillo*, rarer *thraex*
Laquerarius	Lasso, spear and dagger.	(?)	*Secutor* (?)
Myrmillo	Helmet with a crest in the shape of a fish fin, short greave on the left leg, *manica* arm-guard on the right arm, large *scutum* shield, *gladius* sword.	Mid-1st century BC–end of gladiatorial games	*Thraex*, rarer *hoplomachus*
Paegniarius	Quilted wrappings on the legs, left arm and probably head; whip and stick.	1st–3rd centuries AD	*Paegniarius*
Provocator	Helmet, *manica* arm-guard, *cardiophylax* chest-guard, short greave on the left leg, large shield and *gladius* sword.	Late Republican–Imperial period	*Provocator*

Retiarius	Net, trident, dagger, *manica* arm-guard and *galerus* shoulder-guard on the left arm.	Early 1st century AD—end of gladiatorial games	*Secutor*
Sagittarius	Composite bow, conical helmet, scale armour.	(?)	*Sagittarius*
Samnis	Helmet, large shield, spear, sword, greave on the left leg, and probably three-disc armour.	Late 4th century BC—mid-1st century AD	*Samnis* (?)
Secutor	Close-fitting helmet completely covering the head, large rectangular *scutum* shield, *gladius* sword, greave on the left leg, *manica* arm-guard.	Early 1st century AD—end of gladiatorial games	*Retiarius*
Thraex	Helmet, high greaves, small rectangular shield, *manica* arm-guard, curved *sica* dagger.	Early 1st century BC—end of gladiatorial games	*Myrmillo*, rarer *hoplomachus*
Veles	Javelins, sword and shield (?).	Republican period	*Veles* (?)
Venator	Spear.	2nd century BC—AD 681	Animals

MOST COMMON PAIRS OF GLADIATORS

Period	Pairs of gladiators	
1st century BC	*gallus—gallus* (?) *samnis—samnis* (?) *myrmillo—thraex*	*myrmillo—hoplomachus* *eques—eques*
1st century AD	*myrmillo—thraex* *myrmillo—hoplomachus* *retiarius—secutor*	*essedarius—essedarius* *eques—eques*
2nd century AD	*retiarius—secutor* *myrmillo—thraex* *myrmillo—hoplomachus* *essedarius—essedarius* *eques—eques*	*provocator—provocator* (east of the empire) *arbelas—arbelas* (east of the empire) *arbelas—retiarius* (east of the empire)
3rd century AD	*retiarius—secutor* *myrmillo thraex* *myrmillo—hoplomachus* *essedarius—essedarius* *eques—eques*	*provocator—provocator* (east of the empire) *arbelas—arbelas* (east of the empire) *arbelas—retiarius* (east of the empire)
4th century AD	*retiarius—secutor* *myrmillo—thraex*	*myrmillo—hoplomachus* *eques—eques*

GLOSSARY

Ad digitum	'Before the finger is up' or 'before the decision is taken'. Today's meaning is to fight until one side admits defeat.
Amator	Fan, admirer.
Amphitheatrum	Amphitheatre, an elliptically shaped building designed to hold gladiatorial games.
Andabata (pl. andabatae)	A gladiator who fought 'blind', wearing a helmet that had no apertures for eyes.
Arbelas (pl. arbelases; Greek αρβηλας)	Gladiator armed with a distinctive weapon that had a crescent-shaped blade.
Arena (harena)	Sand-sprinkled ground in the amphitheatre on which gladiatorial combat, *venatio* and other performances took place.
Arenarius	Attendant in the arena.
Arma lusoria	'Toy', probably wooden weapon used in *prolusio*.
Armamentarium	Armoury, arsenal.
Auctoratus (pl. auctorati)	Voluntary gladiator. A man who volunteered to become gladiator, signing a contract to do so.
Balteus	Gladiator's belt, as well as the wall in an amphitheatre that partitioned seats earmarked for different social classes.
Bestiarius (pl. bestiarii)	Assistant working with animals in various kinds of *venatio*.
Biga	Chariot with two shaft horses.

Bustuarius (pl. bustuarii)	Gladiator fighting at funeral games in honour of a deceased person.
Caestus	Leather boxer's glove woven from leather belts and often strengthened with leather or metal knuckles.
Carcer	Premises running around the arena behind the *podium* wall.
Cardiophylax	Metal plate protecting a *provocator*'s chest.
Cavea	Seats in the amphitheatre, as well as the spectators as a whole.
Cena libera	Feast given for the participants in a gladiatorial performance on the eve of the games.
Cingulum	Belt made of ring buckles.
Circus	Structure and track for chariot races.
Compositio	Selection of gladiatorial pairs; it was usually done by the *editor* in agreement with the *lanista* and *doctores*.
Confector	Attendant in the arena who finished off wounded animals.
Contraretiarius (pl. contraretiarii)	See *secutor*.
Crista	Plume made of feathers or horsehair.
Crupellarius (pl. crupellarii)	Gladiator wearing very heavy iron armour.
Damnatus ad bestias	Sentenced to be torn to pieces by animals.
Damnatus ad gladium	Sentenced to be killed with a sword.
Damnatus ad ludum	Sentenced to be a gladiator.
Dictata	Combat rules.
Diludium	Break, intermission between combats.
Dimachaerus (pl. dimachaeri; Greek διμαχαιρος)	Gladiator fighting with two swords or daggers.
Doctor (pl. doctores)	Gladiators' trainer in a gladiatorial school.
Edicta muneris	Announcement, notification about gladiatorial games.
Editor	Organizer of gladiatorial games. It was he who, whenever the emperor was absent, decided the fate of the defeated combatants and shaped the repertoire of the games.

Eques (pl. equites)	Type of mounted gladiator who fought with a spear when on horseback and with a sword when on foot. His defensive equipment comprised a broad-brimmed helmet without a crest, *manica* arm-guard on the right arm and a round medium-size shield.
Essedarius (pl. essedarii)	Gladiator who possibly fought in a war chariot, but most likely only on entering the arena, thereafter fighting on foot. His armament included a sword, oval shield and a brimless helmet.
Euripus	Ditch dug on the outer side of the race track in the circus, designed for the protection of the spectators when a *venatio* was held in the building.
Falx	'Sickle, scythe', crescent-shaped weapon of the Dacians. This term was sometimes applied to a *thraex*' sica.
Familia gladiatoria	Group of gladiators under one name. Usually coming from the same school, they were called after the name of the owner of the school.
Familia venatoria	Group of *venatores* under one name. Usually coming from the same school, they were called after the name of the owner of the school.
Fasciae, fasciae crurales	Leg-wrappings, quilted cloth protection for legs.
Ferrum acutum	Sharp (real combat) weapons; compare *arma lusoria*.
Fuscina	Trident of a *retiarius*.
Galea	Helmet.
Galerus	Shoulder-guard worn by the *retiarius* or *laquerarius*. Its turned-out upper edge provided protection for the neck and, to some degree, for the head from sideward blows.
Gallus (pl. galli)	Gaul. One of the early types of gladiator. The term derives from Celts (Gauls), the name of a people conquered by the Romans.
Gladiatrici	Female gladiator.

Gladius	Sword with a straight blade, the weapon of Roman legionaries and some types of gladiator. It is from *gladius* that the term 'gladiator' derives.
Gregarium	Gladiator participating in mass battles.
Gregatim	Mass gladiatorial battle.
Hoplomachus (pl. hoplomachi)	Type of gladiator armed with a spear and sword or dagger and protected with a helmet, high greaves, *manica* and a small round shield.
Hordearius (pl. hordearii)	'Barley-eater', gladiator's nickname.
Hypogeum	Premises under the arena, with stores, cages with animals, lifts and so on.
Jaculator	Another name for a *retiarius*.
Jaculum	'Projectile', net (same meaning as *rete*).
Lanista (pl. lanistae)	Private entrepreneur preparing gladiators in a gladiatorial school and then lending or selling them to an *editor*.
Laquerarius (pl. laquerarii)	Gladiator equipped like a *retiarius* but having a lasso instead of a net.
Leporarium	Enclosure for wild animals.
Libellus munerarius	Programme of gladiatorial combats (written or spoken), providing the names of gladiators in each pair and the order of their appearance in the arena.
Liberatio	Act freeing a gladiator from the obligation to fight in the arena.
Locus (pl. loca)	Seat in the amphitheatre.
Ludia	Dancer, actress; wife of a gladiator.
Ludius	Gladiator, circus fighter.
Ludus (pl. ludi)	Common name for the games as well as a training school for gladiators.
Lusorius	Gladiator fighting with wooden weapons (*arma lusoria*) at the opening of spectacles (during *prolusio*).
Magister	Same as *doctor*.
Manica (pl. manicae)	Leather, cloth or, later, metal arm-guard.

Manumissio	Same as *liberatio*.
Mappa	1. A piece of brightly coloured cloth that *bestiarii* used for teasing animals. 2. A piece of white cloth that the organizer of the games threw on the race track as a signal to start a race.
Meridiana	Second-class fighters.
Minister	Attendant in the arena.
Missilia	Various gifts (food, coins, pearls, and so on) thrown out to the crowds.
Missio	Decision taken by the spectators to spare a defeated gladiator's life; unlike *sine missione* combats, in which one of the gladiators was doomed to die in the arena.
Monomachos (Greek μονομαχοζ)	'single-combat fighter', a common name for a gladiator in the Hellenistic East. The names of different types of gladiator were not usually translated there but transliterated: for example, *secutor* to σεχουτωρ.
Munerarius	Organizer of gladiatorial games.
Munus (pl. munera)	Gladiatorial combat.
Myrmillo or murmillo (pl. myrmillones)	Type of gladiator whose armament consisted of a helmet, a short greave on the left leg, a *manica* arm-guard on the right arm, a *scutum* shield and a *gladius* straight sword.
Naumachia	Mock naval battle, like a gladiatorial contest.
Noxii	Criminals condemned to death, who were either executed or forced to fight in the arena to the death.
Ocrea (pl. ocreae)	Greave.
Oppugnatio	'Attack, siege', combat between a *retiarius* and two *secutores* for the platform (*pons*).
Paegniarius (pl. paegniarii)	Type of gladiator entertaining the public in the intervals between serious fighting. A *paegniarius* was armed with a whip and stick and protected his legs, left arm and possibly his head with quilted wrappings.
Palus	Pole for practising sword blows.

Parma equestris	Small round shield used by the cavalry in Republican Rome as well as by *equites*
Parmula	Small shield used by the *thraex* and *hoplomachus*.
Parmularius (pl. parmularii)	Admirer ('fan') of gladiators who use a small shield.
Pectorale	Same meaning as *cardiophylax*.
Pinnae	'Feathers', a couple of feathers stuck on the sides of a helmet.
Podium	First row of seats in the amphitheatre earmarked for the most notable spectators; the wall of the *podium* formed a barrier round the arena.
Pollice verso	'Death verdict', a refusal to spare the defeated gladiator's life.
Pompa	Ceremonial procession preceding gladiatorial games.
Pons	Platform.
Pontarius (pl. pontarii)	Gladiator fighting on the *pons*. A *retiarius* and two *secutores* were usually in combat there.
Praemium	Monetary reward for a victorious gladiator.
Primus palus	High-ranking gladiator.
Probatio armorum	A check of weapons before combat.
Prolusio	Gladiatorial combat with blunt weapons, held as a prelude to combat with real weapons.
Provocator (pl. provocatores)	Type of gladiator whose armament consisted of a helmet, *manica* arm-guard, *cardiophylax* chest-guard, greave on the left leg, large shield and a *gladius* sword.
Pugio	Dagger.
Rete	*Retiarius'* net.
Retiarius (pl. retiarii)	Type of gladiator whose armament comprised a trident, dagger and net (*rete*); his left arm was protected with a *manica* arm-guard and a *galerus* shoulder-guard.
Rudiarius	Gladiator who received a *rudis* when he was granted his freedom.

Rudis	Stick or wooden sword, an analogue of the *gladius*, used in training and also as a symbol of freedom granted to a gladiator.
Sagittarius (pl. sagittarii)	Gladiator armed with a composite bow, conical helmet and scale armour.
Samnis	Type of gladiator that only existed in the Republican period; equipment is uncertain.
Secunda rudis	'Second stick', umpire's assistant.
Secutor (pl. secutores)	Type of gladiator also known as *contraretiarius*. His equipment was like that of a *myrmillo*, with an essential difference though: his helmet closely fitted his head and face, offering minimal opportunities for a successful attack with a *retiarius*' trident or net.
Sica	Short curved dagger of a *thraex*.
Sine missione	Encounter in which a defeated gladiator could expect no mercy as one of the combatants was to die in the arena.
Scaeva	Left-handed gladiator.
Scissor (pl. scissores)	Same as *arbelas*.
Scutarius (pl. scutarii)	Admirer ('fan') of gladiators with a large shield.
Scutum	Large, 100–120cm high and 65–75cm broad, wooden, leather- or felt-covered shield used by Roman legionaries and some types of gladiators.
Sparsio	Dispersing of aroma.
Spatha	Long sword used in the late Roman Army. The blade was usually 70.5cm long, but some blades are as long as 85cm.
Spatharius (pl. spatharii)	Gladiator armed with a *spatha* sword instead of *gladius*. *Myrmillones-spatharii*, *provocatores-spatharii* and *thracians-spatharii* are known to have existed.
Spectacula	Earlier name for an amphitheatre.
Spina	Vertical rib of a shield.
Spoliarium	Morgue, mortuary, to which slain gladiators were brought. They were stripped of their

armour and those who were still alive were finished off. The *spoliarium* was at the end of the main axis of the amphitheatre, exactly opposite the door through which gladiators entered the arena in a *pompa* at the beginning of the performance.

Stans missus	A gladiatorial combat ending in a draw. Both opponents left the arena on foot.
Strophium	Band for the chest (a sort of a bodice) worn by female gladiators to cover their breasts.
Subligaculum	Gladiator's loincloth.
Summa rudis	'First stick', umpire.
Suppositicius	'Fresh' gladiator who was to fight with an already tired gladiator who had just achieved a victory.
Tertiarius	Same as *suppositicius*.
Thraex	Thracian. Type of gladiator whose armament consisted of a helmet, high greaves, small rectangular shield and *manica* arm-guard. A curved *sica* dagger was his weapon.
Tiro	Novice gladiator.
Velarium or velum	Awning made of strips of cloth fastened on masts that protected spectators from the sun or bad weather. The *velarium* was manipulated by specially recruited sailors who moved it back and forth with the changing position of the sun.
Veles (pl. velites)	Lightly armed gladiator whose main weapon was probably a javelin.
Venabulum	Hunting spear, used by *venatores* for fighting with animals.
Venatio or venationes	'Hunt', entertainment featuring the demonstration of exotic animals or setting beasts on each other or on people.
Venator (pl. venatores)	'Hunter', a gladiator fighting with animals.
Vivarium	Menagerie.

NOTES

INTRODUCTION

1   Junkelmann, *Das Spiel mit dem Tod* (Mainz am Rhein, 2000), p.15.

CHAPTER 1

2   The error was based on the mistaken opinion of the authors of the 2nd–3rd century AD: Tertullianus (*De Spectaculis*, 5.6) and Athenaeus (4.153), whose words were taken as truth, without verification, by many scholars.

3   Junkelmann, *Das Spiel mit dem Tod*, p.33.

4   Livy, 9.40.17.

5   Ville, *La gladiature en occident des origines à la mort de Domitien* (Rome, 1981), pp.1–42.

6   Livy referred to it in Book 16, which does not survive.

7   Tertullianus, *De Spectaculis*, 12.1–4.

8   Livy, 23.30.15.

9   Ibid, 21.42.4–43.1.

10   Ibid, 28.21.1–10.

11   Ibid, 39.46.2.

12   Ibid, 41.28.11.

13   Auguet, *Cruelty and Civilization. The Roman Games* (London & New York, 1994), p.19.

14   Grant, *Gladiators* (New York, 1995), p.12.

15 Köhne 'Bread and Circuses: The Politics of Entertainment', in Eckart Köhne and Cornelia Ewigleben (eds), *Gladiators and Caesars* (London, 2000), p.16.

16 Junkelmann, *Das Spiel mit dem Tod*, pp.38–9.

17 Appian, *Roman History*, 6.72.

18 Tacitus, *Germania*, 10.

19 Livy, 41.20.11–13.

20 Suetonius, *Tiberius*, 37.3.

21 Because the history of Spartacus' insurrection has no immediate connection with the subject of this book and, is well elucidated in literature, I shall confine myself to a brief mention of the main events. To those wanting a detailed knowledge of the subject I would recommend Appian, *Civil Wars*, 13.116–120; Plutarch, *Crassus*, 8–11.

22 Plutarch, *Caesar*, 5.

23 Suetonius, *Caesar*, 26.2 and 39.1; Plutarch, *Crassus*, 55; Coarelli 'Ludus gladiatorius', in Adriano La Regina (ed.), *Sangue e Arena* (Rome, 2001), p.147.

24 Suetonius, *Caesar*, 39.3. Appian (*Civil Wars*, 14.102) gives somewhat different figures: 1,000 infantrymen, 200 riders and 20 elephants on each side.

25 Suetonius, *Augustus*, 43.1.

26 *Res Gestae*, 22.

27 Tacitus, *Annals*, 1.76.

28 Suetonius, *Tiberius*, 7.1.

29 In future date references, when 'BC' is not indicated the date refers to AD.

30 Suetonius, *Caligula*, 18.1.

31 Ibid, 27.1–4 and 35.2.

32 Suetonius, *Claudius*, 21.4–5.

33 Ibid, 34.1-2.

34 Ibid, 21, 6.

35 Suetonius, *Nero*, 11.12; *Domitian*, 4.1; Höfling, *Römer, Sklaven, Gladiatoren. Spartakus vor den Toren Roms* (Moscow, 1992), p.91.

36 Flavius, *Jewish War*, 7.3.1.

37 Seneca, *Moral Epistles to Lucilius*, 7.3–5.

38 Tacitus, *Histories*, 2.95.

39 Ibid, 2.67.

40 Suetonius, *Domitian*, 4.1.

41 The earliest evidence of women taking part in gladiatorial games refers to the time of Nero.

42 Suetonius, *Domitian*, 4.1.

43 Ibid, 17.2.

44 Rea, 'Il Colosseo, teatro per gli spettacoli di caccia. Le fonti e i reperti', in Adriano La Regina (ed.), *Sangue e Arena* (Rome, 2001), p.229.

45 Grant, *Gladiators*, p.36; Höfling, *Römer, Sklaven, Gladiatoren*, p.53.

46 *Historiae Augustae, Hadrian*, 7.12; 9.9.

47 *Historiae Augustae, Marcus Aurelius*, 4.8; 11.4; 27.6; Marcus Aurelius, *Meditations*, 1.5

48 Ibid, 23.5.

49 *Historiae Augustae, Marcus Aurelius*, 8.12; *Historiae Augustae, Verus*, 4.9.

50 *Historiae Augustae, Elagabalus*, 25.7–8.

51 *Historiae Augustae, Marcus Aurelius*, 19.1–7.

52 *Historiae Augustae, Commodus*, 2.9; 10.10–12; 12.12; 13.3–4; 15.3–8.

53 Herodianus, 1.15.

54 *Historiae Augustae, Three Gordians* 3.5.

55 *Historiae Augustae, Maximus and Balbinus*, 8.4–7.

56 *Historiae Augustae, Three Gordians*, 33.1–3.

57 Ibid, 12.3–4.

58 *Historiae Augustae, Probus*, 19.8.

59 Vismara, 'La giornata di spettacoli', in Adriano La Regina (ed.), *Sangue e Arena* (Rome, 2001), p.221; Gregori, 'Aspetti sociali della gladiatura romana', in Adriano La Regina (ed.), *Sangue e Arena* (Rome, 2001), p.25.

60 Grant, *Gladiators*, p.123; Höfling, *Römer, Sklaven, Gladiatoren*, p.117.

61 Some historians believe that the story of the monk Telemachus is no more than a legend, while others argue that the incident actually took place in 391 and that the name of the victim was Almachus. See Höfling, *Römer. Sklaven. Gladiatoren*, p.118; Grant, *Gladiators*, p.123.

62 Durant, *Caesar and Christ* (Moscow, 1995), p.420; Auguet, *Cruelty and Civilization*, p.92.

63 For example, Auguet, *Cruelty and Civilization*, p.93.

64   Junkelmann ('Familia Gladiatoria: The Heroes of the Amphitheatre',
     in Eckart Köhne and Cornelia Ewigleben (eds), *Gladiators and Caesars*
     (London, 2000), p.71) and Iacopi ('Il passaggio sotterraneo cosiddetto
     di Commodo', in Adriano La Regina (ed.), *Sangue e Arena* (Rome, 2001),
     pp.84–5) seem to be of the same general opinion about the role of the
     bestiarius, although there are some differences in detail.

65   Plinius Secundus, *Natural History*, 8.70.182; Ritti and Yilmaz, 'Gladiatori
     e Venationes a Hierapolis di Frigia', *Atti della Accademia Nazionale dei Lincei*,
     Series IX, Vol. X, No. 4 (1998), p.464.

66   Ritti and Yilmaz, 'Gladiatori e Venationes a Hierapolis di Frigia', pp.456–7.

67   Ibid, pp.458–9.

68   Auguet, *Cruelty and Civilization*, p.116.

69   Vismara, 'La giornata di spettacoli', p.207; Durant, *Caesar and Christ*, p.421.

70   Vismara, 'La giornata di spettacoli', p.207.

71   They are described most vividly in Martialis' *Epigrams*.

72   Martialis, *Epigrams*, 7.

73   Ibid, 21.

74   Suetonius, *Nero*, 12.1.

75   Suetonius, *Caligula*, 27.3–4.

76   *Historiae Augustae, Caracalla*, 1.5.

77   Vismara, 'La giornata di spettacoli', p.204.

78   Livy, 39.22.2.

79   Rea, 'Gli animali per la venatio: cattura, trasporto, custodia', in Adriano
     La Regina (ed.), *Sangue e Arena* (Rome, 2001), p.246.

80   Livy, 44.18.8.

81   Rea, 'Gli animali per la venatio: cattura, trasporto, custodia', p.246.

82   *Res Gestae*, 22.

83   Suetonius, *Caligula*, 27.1–4.

84   Suetonius, *Claudius*, 34.2.

85   Ibid, 21.2–3.

86   *Historiae Augustae, Commodus*, 10.2; 12.12; 13.3; Köhne, 'Bread and Circuses:
     The Politics of Entertainment', p.26.

87   Herodianus, 1.15.

88   Marcellinus, 31.10.18.

89   Suetonius, *Titus*, 7.3; Dio, 66.25.4.

90   Flavius, *Jewish War*, 7.3.1.

91   *Historiae Augustae, Hadrian*, 19.2–3 and 7.

92   *Historiae Augustae, Antoninus Pius*, 10.9.

93   *Historiae Augustae, Three Gordians*, 3.5.

94   *Historiae Augustae, Probus*, 19.2–7.

95   *Historiae Augustae, Marcus Aurelius*, 17.7.

96   Ibid, 15.1.

97   Suetonius, *Augustus*, 45.1.

98   *Historiae Augustae, Carus, Carinus and Numerian*, 19.1–2.

99   Rea, 'Il Colosseo, teatro per gli spettacoli di caccia', pp.235–39.

100 Orlandi, 'I loca del Colosseo', in Adriano La Regina (ed.), *Sangue e Arena* (Rome, 2001), p.97.

101 Dio, 61.9; Suetonius, *Nero*, 12.1.

102 Suetonius, *Domitian*, 4.1.

103 Suetonius, *Caesar*, 39.4.

104 *Res Gestae*, 23; Grant, *Gladiators*, p.89; Höfling, *Römer, Sklaven, Gladiatoren*, p.92.

105 Dio, 66.25.4.

106 Fucine Lake is about 150km from Rome.

107 Tacitus, *Annals*, 12.56.

108 Suetonius, *Claudius*, 21.6. It should be noted that the Suetonian original is somewhat different from the wording accepted later – it is addressed to 'emperor' instead of 'Caesar': 'Ave imperator, morituri te salutant!'

109 Suetonius, *Domitian*, 4.2.

110 Grant, *Gladiators*, p.91.

111 *Historiae Augustae, Elagabalus*, 23.1.

112 Grant, *Gladiators*, p.91; Höfling, *Römer, Sklaven, Gladiatoren*, p.95.

113 *Historiae Augustae, Aurelian*, 34.6.

CHAPTER 2

114 Junkelmann, *Das Spiel mit dem Tod* (Mainz am Rhein, 2000), pp.111–2.

115 Ritti and Yilmaz, 'Gladiatori e Venationes a Hierapolis di Frigia', *Atti della Accademia Nazionale dei Lincei*, Series IX, Vol. X, No. 4 (1998), p.478.

116 Artemidorus, *Oneirocritica (The Interpretations of Dreams)*, 2.32.

117 For the supposition of it being a tunic (or chiton) see Ritti and Yilmaz, 'Gladiatori e Venationes a Hierapolis di Frigia', pp.469–79.

118 In his reconstruction, Junkelmann (*Das Spiel mit dem Tod*, p.111) covers the *scissor*'s right arm with a quilted *manica* and his left arm with a metal laminar structure, but the presence of a *manica* on the left arm is contrary to iconographic artefacts.

119 I. V. Akilov, in a private talk.

120 It is only on the basis of an exact reconstruction that conclusions can be made about the total weight of the equipment. Up until recently this work has only been carried out by Junkelmann, yet the data presented in his two works (*Das Spiel mit dem Tod* and 'Familia Gladiatoria: The Heroes of the Amphitheatre' in Eckart Köhne and Cornelia Ewigleben (eds), *Gladiators and Caesars*, London, 2000) vary for some reason. Here I use the smallest figures, which in my opinion are closer to reality as well as to the total weight deduced by simply adding together the weights of the separate items of arms and armour.

121 Grant (*Gladiators*, (New York, 1995) p.62) mentions one more relief (from Amisus), which in his opinion represents a combat between two *dimachaeri* armed with two daggers each.

122 Junkelmann, *Das Spiel mit dem Tod*, p.127; Ritti and Yilmaz, 'Gladiatori e Venationes a Hierapolis di Frigia', p.481.

123 Artemidorus, *Oneirocritica*, 2.32.

124 Ritti and Yilmaz, 'Gladiatori e Venationes a Hierapolis di Frigia', p.480.

125 Junkelmann, *Das Spiel mit dem Tod*, p.110.

126 Marcus Aurelius, *Meditations*, 1.5.

127 Suetonius, *Domitian*, 10.1.

128 I. V. Akilov, in a private talk.

129 The famous mosaic from Zliten (*c.* AD 200) shows two *provocatores* wearing helmets with a low crest and a plume. They look very much like *myrmillones* and are sometimes confused with or mistaken for the latter; however, a high greave on the left leg and the clearly visible belts of the breastplates, crossed on the back, are evidence of their being *provocatores*. Today it is the only

representation of a *provocator* wearing a helmet with a plume. All the other representations show neither a crest nor plume.

130 Robert, *Les gladiateurs dans l'Orient grec* (Paris, 1940), 92f, Nr. 30.

131 Suetonius, *Caligula*, 30.3.

132 Grant, *Gladiators*, p.61.

133 Tacitus, *Annals*, 3.43.

134 Ibid, 3.46.

135 Junkelmann, *Das Spiel mit dem Tod*, p.83.

136 Coarelli, 'L'armamento e le classi dei gladiatori', in Adriano La Regina (ed.), *Sangue e Arena* (Rome, 2001), p.153.

137 Suetonius, *Caligula*, 26.5.

138 Livy, 9.40.17.

139 Ibid, 9.40.2–3.

140 Connolly, *Greece and Rome at War* (Moscow, 2000), p.109.

141 It is depicted on a wine glass from Trierer.

142 Junkelmann, *Das Spiel mit dem Tod*, p.117.

143 Ibid, pp.117–8, 153. Junkelmann draws his conclusion on the basis of a pair of graffiti from Pompeii; however, apart from a spear nothing but a large oval shield and possibly a couple of feathers on the head are visible – there is no actual mention of *essedarii* throwing javelins. Furthermore, the images could represent a *samnis* as well.

144 Isidore of Seville, *Etymologiae*, 18.57; Junkelmann, *Das Spiel mit dem Tod*, p.128.

145 Rostovtsev, *Antichnaya dekorativnaya zhivopis' na yuge Rossii* (St Petersburg, 1913), pp.346–75, tabl. LVXXXIX–XCI.

CHAPTER 3

146 Two samples weighing 6.4 and 6.8kg (14 and 15lb) are known, but their extraordinary heavy weight can be explained by inadequate restoration work, which was carried out in the 19th century. Junkelmann, *Das Spiel mit dem Tod*, (Mainz am Rhein, 2000), pp.72–3.

147 Junkelmann, *Das Spiel mit dem Tod*, p.73.

148 Ibid, p.72.

149 Ritti and Yilmaz, 'Gladiatori e Venationes a Hierapolis di Frigia', *Atti della Accademia Nazionale dei Lincei*, Series IX, Vol. X, No. 4 (1998), p.467.

150 Wisdom, *Gladiators, 100 BC–AD 200* (Oxford, 2001), p.29.

151 Junkelmann, *Das Spiel mit dem Tod*, p.89.

152 Gorelik, *Oruzhie drevnego Vostoka* (St Petersburg, 2003), p.112; Gorelik, 'Zashchitnoe vooruzhenie persov i midyan ahemenidskogo vremeni', in *Vestnik Drevnei Istorii*, No. 3 (1982), p.95. In the Hellenistic epoch these types of arm-guards were already widespread in the Hellenistic East and its outskirts.

153 Robinson, *The Armour of Imperial Rome* (London, 1975), p.160.

154 Wisdom, *Gladiators*, pp.27–8.

155 Junkelmann, *Das Spiel mit dem Tod*, p.90.

156 Ibid, pp.87–9.

157 Connolly, *Greece and Rome at War* (Moscow, 2000), p.131.

158 Ibid, p.233. The reconstructions of a rectangular *scutum* on the basis of a shield from Dura Europos weighs 5.5–7.5kg (12–16.5lb).

159 Junkelmann, *Das Spiel mit dem Tod*, p.79.

160 I. V. Akilov, in a private talk.

161 As real examples of only *hoplomachus'* shields survive, all the other data in the table is approximate. They are based on the reconstructed shields from the Fayum Oasis, La-Tène and Dura Europos, plus their comparison with iconography and a calculated relationship between size and weight.

162 Junkelmann, *Das Spiel mit dem Tod*, p.79.

163 Ibid, p.81.

164 Ibid, p.93.

165 Wisdom, *Gladiators*, p.49.

166 Tumolesi, *Epigrafia anfiteatrale dell'Occidente romano* (Rome, 1988), 62f, No. 59 and 53f, No. 45; Coarelli, 'L'armamento e le classi dei gladiatori', in Adriano La Regina (ed.), *Sangue e Arena* (Rome, 2001), p.155.

167 Junkelmann, *Das Spiel mit dem Tod*, p.92.

168 Ibid, p.95; Junkelmann, 'Familia Gladiatoria: The Heroes of the Amphitheatre', in Eckart Köhne and Cornelia Ewigleben (eds), *Gladiators and Caesars* (London, 2000), p.60 (in different works Junkelmann gives different weights for the net).

169 Kanz and Grossschmidt, 'Head injuries of Roman gladiators', *Forensic Science International*, Vol. 160, No. 2 (2006), pp.3, 9.

170 Wisdom, *Gladiators*, p.23.

171 Junkelmann, *Das Spiel mit dem Tod*, p.53; Junkelmann, 'Familia Gladiatoria: The Heroes of the Amphitheatre', p.47.

172 Wisdom, *Gladiators*, p.29.

173 Juvenalis, *Satires*, 8.200–210.

174 Suetonius, *Caligula*, 30.3.

CHAPTER 4

175 Dio, 72.19.4; Junkelmann, *Das Spiel mit dem Tod*, (Mainz am Rhein, 2000), p.128.

176 Marcialis, *Epigrams*, 5.24.

177 Höfling, *Römer, Sklaven, Gladiatoren. Spartakus vor den Toren Roms* (Moscow, 1992), p.101.

178 Kanz and Grossschmidt, 'Head injuries of Roman gladiators', *Forensic Science International*, Vol. 160, No. 2 (2006), pp.207–16.

179 Tertullianus, *Apology*, 15.4.

180 Lucian, *Toxaris or Friendship*, 59.60.

181 Artemidorus, *Oneirocritica (The Interpretations of Dreams)*, 2.32.

CHAPTER 5

182 Vitruvius, 1.7.1.

183 *Res Gestae*, 22.

184 Plinius Secundus, *Natural History*, 36.24.117–20.

185 For example, Ovidius (*Metamorphoses*, 11.25), mentioning the chase of a deer, speaks about a 'two-sided theatre'.

186 Tacitus, *Annals*, 4.62–63; Suetonius, *Tiberius*, 40.

187 Suetonius, *Caligula*, 21.

188 Tacitus, *Annals*, 13.31; Suetonius, *Nero*, 12.

189 The name Colosseum is first mentioned in the 7th century.

190 Junkelmann, *Das Spiel mit dem Tod*, (Mainz am Rhein, 2000), p.21.

191 Grant, *Gladiators*, (New York, 1995), p.88.

192 Auguet, *Cruelty and Civilization. The Roman Games* (London & New York, 1994), pp.207–9.

193 The sand from the Nile was particularly valued.

194 Suetonius, *Caligula*, 18.3; Plinius Secundus, *Natural History*, 33.27.90.

195 This wall is sometimes called the *podium*, although the name should refer only to the seats in the first row of the amphitheatre designed for leading figures. To avoid misunderstanding, we shall use the word *podium* for seats in the pit of the amphitheatre, while the wall surrounding the arena will be called the *podium* wall.

196 Livy, 34.54.4–8.

197 Orlandi, 'I loca del Colosseo', in Adriano La Regina (ed.), *Sangue e Arena* (Rome, 2001), p.89.

198 Suetonius, *Augustus*, 44.1–3; Orlandi, 'I loca del Colosseo', p.89.

199 Suetonius, *Augustus*, 44.

200 Orlandi, 'I loca del Colosseo', pp.90–1.

201 Rea, 'L'anfiteatro di Roma: note strutturali e di funzionamento', in Adriano La Regina (ed.), *Sangue e Arena* (Rome, 2001), p.74.

202 Tacitus, *Annals*, 14.17.

203 Auguet, *Cruelty and Civilization*, p.33.

204 This speed of exit possibly gave the name to exits from amphitheatres and theatres – 'vomitories' (from the Latin *vomitor* – one suffering from vomiting).

205 All these inscriptions date from the 3rd–5th centuries AD. Until the late 3rd century, inscriptions were either made with paint, which did not last, or were not made at all. The omission of inscriptions may be a consequence of the insignificant part played by the Senate under many emperors of the time. The situation changes around the turn of the 3rd century through the early 4th century, when the Senate recovered its political weight. From that time up to the 5th century, the names of senators were carved on the parapet or the cornice of the *podium* opposite the seats assigned to them. Orlandi, 'I loca del Colosseo', p.93.

206 Beste, 'I sotterranei del Colosseo: impianto, transformazioni e funzionamento' in Adriano La Regina (ed.), *Sangue e Arena* (Rome, 2001), p.297.

207 Auguet, *Cruelty and Civilization*, p.41.

208 The architects probably began to built the *hypogeum* as far back as under Emperor Domitian, as the last reference (Suetonius, *Domitian*, 4.1) to naval

battles in the Colosseum dates exactly from the period of Domitian's rule, and there is no later information of *naumachia* being held here.

209 Barbera, 'Un anfiteatro di corte: il Castrense' in Adriano La Regina (ed.), *Sangue e Arena* (Rome, 2001), pp.127–45.

210 Auguet, *Cruelty and Civilization*, pp.202–3.

211 Ibid, p.206; Grant, *Gladiators*, pp.86–7.

212 Mahjoubi, *Villes et structures urbaines de la province romaine d'Afrique* (Tunis, 2000), pp.167–73.

213 Grant, *Gladiators*, pp.86–8.

214 Mahjoubi, *Villes et structures urbaines de la province romaine d'Afrique*, p.164.

CHAPTER 6

215 Gregori, 'Aspetti sociali della gladiatura romana', in Adriano La Regina (ed.), *Sangue e Arena* (Rome, 2001), p.19.

216 Junkelmann, *Das Spiel mit dem Tod*, (Mainz am Rhein, 2000), p.41; Auguet (*Cruelty and Civilization. The Roman Games* (London & New York, 1994), p.178) believes that the price of a veteran gladiator ranged between 500 to 3,000 sesterces depending on the rank of a gladiator, and a *gregarium* was even cheaper.

217 Dio, 54.2.3–4; Gregori, 'Aspetti sociali della gladiatura romana', in Adriano La Regina (ed.), *Sangue e Arena* (Rome, 2001), p.17; Ville, *La gladiature en occident des origines à la mort de Domitien* (Rome, 1981), pp.121–2.

218 Tacitus, *Annals*, 4.63.

219 Gregori, 'Aspetti sociali della gladiatura romana', p.19.

220 Höfling, *Römer, Sklaven, Gladiatoren. Spartakus vor den Toren Roms* (Moscow, 1992), p.61.

221 Tacitus, *Annals*, 13.49.

222 Gregori, 'Aspetti sociali della gladiatura romana', p.18.

223 Ibid, p.18; Tumolesi, *Epigrafia anfiteatrale dell'Occidente romano* (Rome, 1988), pp.127–8.

224 Rea, 'Il Colosseo, teatro per gli spettacoli di caccia. Le fonti e i reperti', in Adriano La Regina (ed.), *Sangue e Arena* (Rome, 2001), p.234.

225 *Historiae Augustae, Aurelian*, 33.4.

226 Vismara, 'La giornata di spettacoli', in Adriano La Regina (ed.), *Sangue e Arena* (Rome, 2001), p.200; Mahjoubi, *Villes et structures urbaines de la province romaine d'Afrique* (Tunis, 2000), p.160.

227 Rea, 'Gli animali per la venatio: cattura, trasporto, custodia', in Adriano La Regina (ed.), *Sangue e Arena* (Rome, 2001), p.253.

228 Ibid, pp.249–50.

229 Ibid, p.251.

230 Ibid, p.258.

231 Plinius Secundus, *Natural History*, 8.21.

232 Rea, 'Gli animali per la venatio: cattura, trasporto, custodia', p.257.

233 Ibid, p.262.

234 Ibid, pp.260–1.

235 Ibid, p.269.

236 Ibid, pp.250–1.

237 Ibid, p.263.

238 Such incidents were mentioned, for instance, by Plinius Secundus (*Natural History*, 36.4.40).

239 Rea, 'Gli animali per la venatio: cattura, trasporto, custodia', p.271.

240 Suetonius, *Claudius*, 21.3.

241 Rea, 'Gli animali per la venatio: cattura, trasporto, custodia', pp.273–4.

242 Coarelli, 'Ludus gladiatorius', in Adriano La Regina (ed.), *Sangue e Arena* (Rome, 2001), p.147.

243 Plutarch, *Crassus*, 8.3.

244 Suetonius, *Caesar*, 26.3.

245 Coarelli, 'Ludus gladiatorius', p.147.

246 Ibid, p.147.

247 Ibid, p.148.

248 Wisdom, *Gladiators, 100 BC–AD 200* (Oxford, 2001), p.21; Höfling, *Römer, Sklaven, Gladiatoren*, p.35.

249 Vegetius, I.11.

250 Grant, *Gladiators* (New York, 1995), p.49.

251 Guhl and Koner, *The Romans. Their Life and Customs* (Twickenham, 1994), p.556.

252 *Historiae Augustae, Hadrian*, 18.8.

253 Grant, *Gladiators*, p.29; Höfling, *Römer, Sklaven, Gladiatoren*, p.22.

254 Tumolesi, *Gladiatorum paria: annuncdi di spettacoli gladiatori a Pompei* (Rome, 1980), pp.100–01; Gregori, 'Aspetti sociali della gladiatura romana', p.21.

255 Grant, *Gladiators*, p.31.

256 'Uri, vinciri, verberari, ferroque necari.' Petronius, *Satyricon*, 117.

257 Ville, *La gladiature en occident des origines à la mort de Domitien* (Rome, 1981), pp.246–55; Gregori, 'Aspetti sociali della gladiatura romana', p.21.

258 Tertullianus, *Ad Mart.*, 5.

259 Lucian, *Toxaris or Friendship*, 59.60.

260 Grant, *Gladiators*, p.32.

261 Junkelmann, *Das Spiel mit dem Tod*, p.24.

262 Grant, *Gladiators*, pp.98–9.

263 Suetonius, *Caligula*, 32.2.

264 *Historiae Augustae, Hadrian*, 14.10; *Didius Julianus*, 9.1; Höfling, *Römer, Sklaven, Gladiatoren*, pp.106–7.

265 *Historiae Augustae, Macrinus*, 4.5.

266 Livy, 28.21.2.

267 Juvenalis, *Satires*, 6.216–17.

268 Gregori, 'Aspetti sociali della gladiatura romana', p.21.

269 Suetonius, *Tiberius*, 35.2.

270 Tacitus, *Histories*, 2.62.

271 Tacitus, *Annals*, 15.32.

272 Grant, *Gladiators*, p.34.

273 Suetonius, *Domitian*, 4.1.

274 Juvenalis, *Satires*, 6.247–63.

275 Gregori, 'Aspetti sociali della gladiatura romana', p.24.

276 Ewigleben, '"What these Women Love is the Sword": The Performers and their Audiences' in Eckart Köhne and Cornelia Ewigleben (eds), *Gladiators and Caesars* (London, 2000), p.127; Höfling, *Römer, Sklaven, Gladiatoren*, p.33; Burton, *The Book of the Sword* (New York, 1987), p.250.

277 Juvenalis, *Satires*, 3.36.

278 Suetonius, *Augustus*, 45.3.

279 Ville, *La gladiature en occident des origines à la mort de Domitien*, pp.318–25.

280 Höfling, *Römer, Sklaven, Gladiatoren*, p.110.

281 Ville, *La gladiature en occident des origines à la mort de Domitien*, p.321; Junkelmann, *Das Spiel mit dem Tod*, p.145; Junkelmann, 'Familia Gladiatoria: The Heroes of the Amphitheatre', in Eckart Köhne and Cornelia Ewigleben (eds), *Gladiators and Caesars* (London, 2000), p.70.

282 Grant, *Gladiators*, p.77; Wisdom, *Gladiators*, pp.46–7.

283 Seneca, *Epistles*, 70.26; 70.23; 70.20.

284 Höfling, *Römer, Sklaven, Gladiatoren*, p.46.

285 Gladiatorial detachments were hired for personal protection not only by many noble Romans, but also by citizens whose ideals ought to have been in opposition to the very existence of gladiators. Thus, in spite of the fact that most Christians came out in favour of the prohibition of gladiatorial games, in 367 Pope Damasus I, at the time of war with the anti-pope Ursinus, recruited a detachment of gladiator bodyguards (Köhne, 2000, p.30).

286 For example, Tacitus, *Annals*, 13.25.

287 Höfling, *Römer, Sklaven, Gladiatoren*, p.49.

288 Tacitus, *Annals*, 3.43.

289 Höfling, *Römer, Sklaven, Gladiatoren*, p.49.

290 Ibid, p.97; Coarelli, 'Ludus gladiatorius', p.147.

291 Appian, *Civil Wars*, 15.49.

292 Tacitus, *Histories*, 2.11.

293 Plutarch, *Otho*, 10–12; Suetonius, *Vitellius*, 15.2; Tacitus, *Histories*, 2.34–35,43. It should be noted, however, that Praetorian Guards proved even worse than the gladiators.

294 Tacitus, *Histories*, 3.77.

295 *Historiae Augustae, Marcus Aurelius*, 21.7; 23.5.

296 *Historiae Augustae, Didius Julianus*, 8.3.

297 Suetonius, *Caligula*, 38.4.

298 Gregori, 'Aspetti sociali della gladiatura romana', pp.22–3.

299 See, for example, Marcus Aurelius, *Meditations*, 1.5.

300 Suetonius, *Caligula*, 55.2; Ville, *La gladiature en occident des origines à la mort de Domitien* (Rome, 1981), p.337.

301 Suetonius, *Nero*, 30.2; Ville, *La gladiature en occident des origines à la mort de Domitien*, p.289.

302 Gregori, 'Aspetti sociali della gladiatura romana', p.24; Ville, *La gladiature en occident des origines à la mort de Domitien*, p.330; Höfling, *Römer, Sklaven, Gladiatoren*, p.101.

303 Tacitus, *Annals*, 11.21; *Historiae Augustae, Marcus Aurelius*, 19.1–7.

304 Juvenalis, *Satires*, 6.109–10.

305 Gregori, 'Aspetti sociali della gladiatura romana', p.22.

CHAPTER 7

306 Martialis (*Spectacles*, 27(29).5) also says that a fight was terminated with the holding up of a finger.

307 Juvenalis, *Satires*, 6.36.

308 Horatius, *Epistles*, 1.18.66.

309 Junkelmann, 'Familia Gladiatoria: The Heroes of the Amphitheatre', in Eckart Köhne and Cornelia Ewigleben (eds), *Gladiators and Caesars* (London, 2000), pp.31, 68.

310 Junkelmann, *Das Spiel mit dem Tod*, (Mainz am Rhein, 2000), pp.138–9.

311 This is a usual interpretation of the terms *pollicem vertere* and *pollice verso*.

312 Velishskii, *Istoriya civilizacii. Byt i nravy drevnih grekov i rimlyan* (Moscow, 2000), p.544.

313 Burton, *The Book of the Sword* (New York, 1987), p.250.

314 Guhl and Koner, *The Romans. Their Life and Customs* (Twickenham, 1994), p.562. A handkerchief is mentioned by Grant, too (*Gladiators*, New York, 1995, p.75); with regard to thumbs, however, he shares the 'traditional' point of view.

315 Suetonius, *Claudius*, 34.1.

316 Cicero, *Tusculan Disputations*, 2.17.41.

317 Servants using red-hot irons or hammers are only mentioned by Tertullianus (*Apology*, 15.4) when he describes a midday performance. There is no iconographic artefact carrying the image of such a costumed person. In one of his works (*Das Spiel mit dem Tod*, pp.140–1), Junkelmann suggests that these customs were only applied to convicts, while in another work ('Familia Gladiatoria: The Heroes of the Amphitheatre', p.68) he questions the existence of the customs in general.

318 Grant, *Gladiators*, p.78. This limitation was introduced by Marcus Aurelius.

BIBLIOGRAPHY

PRIMARY SOURCES

Appian, *Roman History*, Vols I–IV (Cambridge, MA, 1913)

Artemidorus, *Oneirocritica (The Interpretation of Dreams)*, (Park Ridge, 1975)

Artemidorus, *Oneirocritica (The Interpretation of Dreams)*, (St Petersburg, 1999)

Athenaeus, *The Deipnosophists or Banquet of the Learned of Athenaeus* (London, 1854)

Aurelius, Marcus, *Meditations* (Cambridge, MA, 1916)

Cicero, Marcus Tullius, *Izbrannye sochineniya* (Moscow, 2000)

Cicero, Marcus Tullius, *Philosophical Treatises, Tusculan Disputations* (Cambridge, MA, 1927)

Crispus, Gaius Sallustius, *War with Catiline. War with Jugurtha. Selections from the Histories. Doubtful Works* (Cambridge, MA, 1921)

Dio, Cassius, *Dio's Roman History* (Cambridge, 1954)

Dio, Cassius, *Roman History* Vols I–IX (Cambridge, MA, 1914–27)

Flavius, *The Jewish War* (Cambridge, MA, 1927–28)

Gaius, Arbiter Petronius, *Satyricon. Apocolocyntosis* (Cambridge, MA, 1913)

Herodianus, *History of the Empire* (Cambridge, MA, 1969)

Historiae Augustae, Vlasteliny Rima. Biographii rimskih imperatorov ot Adriana do Diokletiana (Scriptores Historiae Augustae) (St Petersburg, 2001)

Historiae Augustae Vols I–III (Cambridge, MA, 1921–32)

Horatius Flaccus, Quintus, *The Complete Works of Horace* (New York, 1936)

Juvenalis, *Juvenal and Persius* (Cambridge, MA, 2004)

Juvenalis, Decimus Junius, *Satiry* (Moscow & Leningrad, 1937)

Livy, *The History of Rome* (London, 1905)

Lucian, *Lucian*, Vols I–VIII (Cambridge, MA, 1913–67)

Marcellinus, Ammianus, *The Later Roman Empire: 354–378* (Harmondsworth, 1969)

Martialis, Marcus Valerius, *Epigrams* Vols I–III (Cambridge, MA, 1993)

Martialis, Marcus Valerius, *Epigrams* (Moscow & Kharkov, 2000)

Nicolaus of Damascus, 'History', *Vestnik Drevnei Istorii*, No. 3–4 (1960)

Nicolaus Damascenus, *Nicolaus Of Damascus' Life Of Augustus: A Historical Commentary Embodying A Translation* (Whitefish, 2007)

Ovidius Naso, Publius, *Metamorphoses* (Cambridge, MA, 1916)

Ovidius Naso, Publius, *Metamorphoses* (St Petersburg, 1994)

Plinius Secundus, *Natural History*, Vols I–X (Cambridge, MA, 1938–62)

Plutarch, *Plutarch's Lives* (London & New York, 1919–20)

Plutarch, *Parallel Lives*, Vols I–XI (Cambridge, MA, 1914–26)

Renatus, Flavius Vegetius, *De Re Militari* (St Petersburg, 1996)

Renatus, Flavius Vegetius, *Epitoma Rei Militaris* (New York, 1990)

Res Gestae Divi Augusti (Cambridge, MA, 1924)

Res Gestae, Res Gestae divi Augusti / Rimskaya Istoriya (Moscow, 1900) pp.40–53

Seneca, Lucius Annaeus, *Moral Epistles*, Vols I–III (Cambridge, MA, 1917–25)

Strabo, *Geography* Vols I–VIII (Cambridge, MA, 1917–32)

Suetonius, *The Lives of the Caesars*, Vols I–II (Cambridge, MA, 1914)

Tranquillus, Gaius Suetonius, *Zhizn' dvenadcati Cesarei* (Moscow, 1988)

Tacitus, Publius Cornelius, *The Annals & The Histories* (London, 1864–1877)

Tacitus, Publius Cornelius, *Agricola. Germania. Dialogue on Oratory* (Cambridge, MA, 1914)

Tertullianus, Quintus Septimius Florens, *Apology and De Spectaculis. Octavius* (Cambridge, MA, 1931)

Vitruvius, *Ten Books on Architecture* (Cambridge, 1999)

SECONDARY SOURCES

Auguet, R., *Cruelty and Civilization. The Roman Games* (London & New York, 1994)

Baracconi, G., *Spettacoli nell' antica Roma* (Rome, 1972)

Barbera, M., 'Un anfiteatro di corte: il Castrense' in Adriano La Regina (ed.), *Sangue e Arena* (Rome, 2001) pp.127–45

Beste, H-J., 'I sotterranei del Colosseo: impianto, transformazioni e funzionamento' in Adriano La Regina (ed.), *Sangue e Arena* (Rome, 2001) pp.277–99

Burton, R. F., *The Book of the Sword* (New York, 1987)

Bussi, S., and Foraboschi, D., 'Spartaco: il personaggio, il mito, la vicenda', in Adriano La Regina (ed.), *Sangue e Arena* (Rome, 2001) pp. 29–41

Coarelli, F., 'Gli anfiteatri a Roma prima del Colosseo' in Adriano La Regina (ed.), *Sangue e Arena* (Rome, 2001) pp.43–47

Coarelli, F., 'Il rilievo con scene gladiatorie (Monumento di Lusius Storax)', *Studi Miscellanei*, No. 10 (1966) pp.85–99

Coarelli, F., 'L'armamento e le classi dei gladiatori', in Adriano La Regina (ed.), *Sangue e Arena* (Rome, 2001) pp.153–73

Coarelli, F., 'Ludus gladiatorius', in Adriano La Regina (ed.), *Sangue e Arena* (Rome, 2001) pp.147–51

Coarelli, F., and Tamassia R., 'Ludi, munera, venationes', in F. M. Ricci (ed.), *Lo Sport nel Mondo Antico* (Milan, 1987) pp.55–59

Connolly, P., *Greece and Rome at War* (Moscow, 2000)

Conti, C., 'Il modello ligneo dell'Anfiteatro Flavio, di Carlo Lucangelli: osservazioni nel corso del restauro', in Adriano La Regina (ed.), *Sangue e Arena* (Rome, 2001) pp.117–25

Coussin, P., 'Guerriers et Gladiateurs samnites', *Revue Archéologique*, Vol. 32 (1930) pp.235–79

Durant, W., *Caesar and Christ* (Moscow, 1995)

Ewigleben, C., '"What these Women Love is the Sword": The Performers and their Audiences' in Eckart Köhne and Cornelia Ewigleben (eds), *Gladiators and Caesars* (London, 2000) pp.125–39

Gorelik, M. V., *Oruzhie drevnego Vostoka* (St Petersburg, 2003)

Gorelik, M. V., 'Zashchitnoe vooruzhenie persov i midyan ahemenidskogo vremeni', *Vestnik Drevnei Istorii*, No. 3 (1982) pp.90–105

Grant, M., *Gladiators* (New York, 1995)

Gregori, G. L., 'Aspetti sociali della gladiatura romana', in Adriano La Regina (ed.), *Sangue e Arena* (Rome, 2001) pp.15–27

Guhl, E., and Koner, W., *The Romans. Their Life and Customs* (Twickenham, 1994)

Höfling, H., *Römer, Sklaven, Gladiatoren. Spartakus vor den Toren Roms* (Moscow, 1992)

Iacopi, I., 'Il passaggio sotterraneo cosiddetto di Commodo', in in Adriano La Regina (ed.), *Sangue e Arena* (Rome, 2001) pp.79–87

Junkelmann, M., *Das Spiel mit dem Tod* (Mainz am Rhein, 2000)

Junkelmann, M., 'Familia Gladiatoria: The Heroes of the Amphitheatre', in Eckart Köhne and Cornelia Ewigleben (eds), *Gladiators and Caesars* (London, 2000) pp.31–74

Kanz, F., and Grossschmidt, K., 'Head injuries of Roman gladiators', *Forensic Science International*, Vol. 160, No. 2 (2006) pp.207–16

Köhne, E., 'Bread and Circuses: The Politics of Entertainment', in Eckart Köhne and Cornelia Ewigleben (eds), *Gladiators and Caesars* (London, 2000) pp.8–30

Kyle, D. G., *Spectacles of Death in Ancient Rome* (London & New York, 1998)

Mahjoubi, A., *Villes et structures urbaines de la province romaine d'Afrique* (Tunis, 2000)

Mannix, D., *Those about to Die* (New York, 1958)

Orlandi, S., 'I loca del Colosseo', in Adriano La Regina (ed.), *Sangue e Arena* (Rome, 2001) pp.89–103

Panella, C., 'La valle del Colosseo prima del Colosseo e la Meta Sudans', in Adriano La Regina (ed.), *Sangue e Arena* (Rome, 2001) pp. 49–67

Pesando, F., 'Gladiatori a Pompei', in Adriano La Regina (ed.), *Sangue e Arena* (Rome, 2001) pp.175–97

Rea, R., 'Gli animali per la venatio: cattura, trasporto, custodia', in Adriano La Regina (ed.), *Sangue e Arena* (Rome, 2001) pp.245–75

Rea, R., 'Il Colosseo, teatro per gli spettacoli di caccia. Le fonti e i reperti', in Adriano La Regina (ed.), *Sangue e Arena* (Rome, 2001) pp.223–43

Rea, R., 'L'anfiteatro di Roma: note strutturali e di funzionamento', in Adriano La Regina (ed.), *Sangue e Arena* (Rome, 2001) pp.69–77

Ritti, T., and Yilmaz, S., 'Gladiatori e Venationes a Hierapolis di Frigia', *Atti della Accademia Nazionale dei Lincei*, Series IX, Vol. X, No. 4 (1998) pp.445–542

Robert, L., *Les gladiateurs dans l'Orient grec* (Paris, 1940)

Robert, L., 'Monuments de gladiateurs dans l'Orient grec', *Hellenica III* (1946) pp.112–50

Robert, L., 'Monuments de gladiateurs dans l'Orient grec', *Hellenica VIII* (1950) pp.39–72

Robinson, R. H., *The Armour of Imperial Rome* (London, 1975)

Rostovtsev, M. I., *Antichnaya dekorativnaya zhivopis' na yuge Rossii* (St Petersburg, 1913)

Schingo, G., 'I modelli del Colosseo' in Adriano La Regina (ed.), *Sangue e Arena* (Rome, 2001) pp.105–15

Schingo, G., 'La documentazione degli scavi napoleonici dell'arena nei rilievi di Luigi Maria Valadier', in Adriano La Regina (ed.), *Sangue e Arena* (Rome, 2001) pp.301–13

Smith, W., *A Dictionary of Greek and Roman Antiquities* (London, 1875)

Tumolesi, Sabbatini P., *Epigrafia anfiteatrale dell'Occidente romano* (Rome, 1988)

Tumolesi, Sabbatini P., 'Gladiatoria', *Atti della Accademia Nazionale dei Lincei*, No. 27 (1973) pp.485–95

Tumolesi, Sabbatini P., *Gladiatorum paria: annuncdi di spettacoli gladiatori a Pompei* (Rome, 1980)

Tumolesi, Sabbatini P., 'Gli spettacoli anfiteatrali alla luce di alcune testimonianze epigrafiche', in M. L. Conforto et. al., *Anfiteatro Flavio. Immagine Testimonianze Spettacoli* (Romae, 1988) pp.91–99

Velishskii, F., *Istoriya civilizacii. Byt i nravy drevnih grekov i rimlyan* (Moscow, 2000)

Ville, G., 'Essai de datation de la mosaïque des Gladiateurs de Zliten', in M. G. Picard & H. Stern (eds.), *Colloques internationaux la mosaïque gréco-romaine* (Paris, 1965) pp.147–55

Ville, G., *La gladiature en occident des origines à la mort de Domitien* (Rome, 1981)

Ville, G., *Recherches sur le costume, l'armament et la technique des Gladiateurs romains*, Académie des Inscriptions et Belles-Lettres, Comptes Rendus des Séances de l'Année (Paris, 1961)

Vismara, C., 'La giornata di spettacoli', in Adriano La Regina (ed.), *Sangue e Arena* (Rome, 2001) pp.199–221

Wisdom, S., *Gladiators, 100 BC–AD 200* (Oxford, 2001)

INDEX

Figures in **bold** refer to illustrations